£6. 99
Pwbls

The Cold War and After

J F AYLETT

Contents

HODDER 20th CENTURY *History*

Hodder & Stoughton
A MEMBER OF THE HODDER HEADLINE GROUP

1945: The End of the War

When the war ended in 1945, most European countries were in ruins or exhausted by six years of fighting. Countries which had once been powerful now needed peace to rebuild themselves. Only two superpowers remained after 1945 – the USA and the USSR.

They had fought the war together as allies. They had shared victory together. Yet, afterwards, they did not completely trust each other. This distrust never led to fighting between the two countries but there were regular quarrels. Historians call this period the 'Cold War'.

The reasons for this distrust went back to long before the Second World War. In 1917, the Russian Revolution had put communists in power in Russia. (They had changed its name to USSR in 1924.) Soon afterwards, countries such as Britain and the USA helped the communists' opponents during a bitter civil war. From then onwards, the Russians did not trust the Americans and the Americans did not trust the Russians.

The Soviet Union wanted to spread communism. American leaders were afraid that the USSR would try to start communist revolutions elsewhere in the world, including in the United States itself.

> Russia had been attacked 14 times since 1800. The city of Minsk had been occupied 101 times.

The USSR's leader was Joseph Stalin. He did not trust the USA or Britain to protect the USSR. It was 1933 before the USA recognised the Soviet Union. For most of the 1930s, neither Britain nor the USA supported him against Hitler. Stalin had become convinced that the West intended to let Hitler destroy the USSR.

Because the USSR was the only communist country, Stalin felt isolated. He believed that capitalist countries might use their money to attack the Soviet Union.

In 1941, the USSR was attacked by a capitalist country – Nazi Germany. The USSR fought alongside the USA and Britain to defeat Hitler but it cost at least 20 million Soviet lives. Stalin was bitter that the western Allies did not invade Europe until 1944. He was still convinced that they wanted to destroy communism.

As his Red Army pushed back the German armies in 1942–5, Stalin was determined that his country would be secure in future. He believed the USSR had to organise its own defence. One way of doing it was to make sure that neighbouring countries were friendly to the USSR, and therefore unlikely to attack her. Stalin decided that meant they had to become communist as well.

In 1945, Britain and the USA could not stop him doing this. By then, nearly all of eastern Europe was under the Red Army's control.

A The differences between the Soviet communist system and the American capitalist system also made the two countries frightened of each other.

COMMUNISM

One-party state: only the Communist Party permitted

All industry and businesses are owned by the state. The government runs the newspapers and the radio

YAKOVICH Communist Party
POKROVSKY Communist Party
STADNIK Communist Party

CAPITALISM

Several political parties: voters may choose

REPUBLICAN
DEMOCRAT

All industry and businesses are privately-owned. So are newspapers and radio stations

B A French cartoon showing Russian foreign policy after the Second World War.

Yalta (February 4–11 1945)

In February 1945, Churchill (representing Britain), President Roosevelt (USA) and Stalin (USSR) held a **summit meeting** at Yalta in the Soviet Union. Stalin wanted the Germans to pay huge **reparations** to cover the damage which the Germans had done in the Soviet Union.

Churchill and Roosevelt did not think it was sensible to punish Germany like this but Stalin was determined. So they agreed that the USSR would get reparations in goods. The Russians took factory equipment and other materials out of Germany and Austria and took them back to the USSR. At the same time, many East Germans were put in labour camps and forced to work for the Russians.

C The other main decisions taken at Yalta were:

1. Germany would be *demilitarised* and divided into four zones, each controlled by one Allied power – the USSR, USA, Britain and France.
2. The city of Berlin would also be divided between the four powers.
3. Eastern Europe should be under Soviet influence.
4. In return, Stalin accepted that Britain would have influence over Greece.
5. The USSR gained land from eastern Poland (up to the Curzon Line). Poland would gain land from Germany in return.
6. Germans who were guilty of war crimes would be put on trial.
7. Countries freed from the Germans could choose their own democratic government in free elections.
8. Stalin agreed to join the new United Nations organisation.
9. The USSR would join in the war against Japan soon after Germany surrendered.

Potsdam (July 17–August 1 1945)

Despite the distrust, Stalin and Roosevelt got on well at Yalta but it was the last time they met. In April 1945, Roosevelt died and Harry Truman became American President. On 7 May 1945, Germany surrendered and the war in Europe ended.

The Allies next met at Potsdam in July 1945. During this conference, Churchill learned that he had lost the General Election. The new Prime Minister, Attlee, took over as British representative on July 27.

Something else happened during the Potsdam Conference. Truman learned that the atomic bomb had been successfully tested. He told Stalin that the USA had developed a new weapon but Stalin may not have realised how important this was. In any case, Truman did not tell Stalin that he was about to drop an atomic bomb on Japan.

D US President Harry Truman later wrote about the conference:

> The personal meeting with Stalin and the Russians enabled me to see at first hand what we and the West had to face in the future. Force is the only thing the Russians understand.

E British PM Clement Attlee also recalled the meeting (1960):

> The Russians had shown themselves even more difficult than anyone expected. After Potsdam, one couldn't be very hopeful any longer. It was quite obvious they were going to be troublesome. The war had left them holding positions far into Europe, much too far. I had no doubt they intended to use them.

Q

1. a) Why did the USA distrust the USSR before Potsdam?
   b) Why did the USSR distrust the USA before Potsdam?
   c) How does this column suggest that Potsdam increased the distrust?
2. a) What did Stalin achieve at the two conferences which would help the USSR's defence?
   b) What did the western Allies achieve?
3. a) Study source B carefully. Do you think Stalin was planning this? Give reasons.
   b) How accurate do you think this cartoon is?

THE USSR AND POLAND

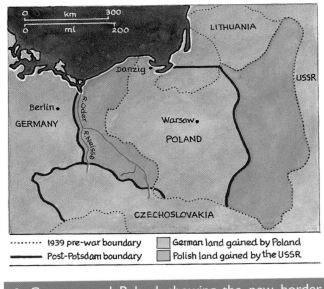

A Germany and Poland, showing the new border, after the Potsdam Conference.

Some new decisions were made at Potsdam. The British and Americans agreed that the USSR could take 25 per cent of the industrial equipment from the western zones of Germany as reparations. They also allowed the USSR to send all Germans living in Poland, Hungary and Czechoslovakia back to Germany.

But the key agreement concerned Poland. At Yalta, Poland's western boundary had not been finally fixed. Before the Potsdam Conference, Stalin privately agreed with the Poles to fix it along the Rivers Oder and Neisse. (It became known as the Oder-Neisse Line.) This was further west than either the Allies or the Germans wanted.

However, Stalin repeated his promise that there would be free elections in Poland. Poland was important because British support for Poland had led to war. Polish elections were held – but they were far from free.

As early as 1941, the USSR had parachuted communists into Poland to fight the fascists and promote communism. Meanwhile, the Polish government had gone into exile in London.

In 1943, there was conflict between the USSR and the Polish government. The USSR broke off all relations with it and set up a rival 'National Committee' in Moscow.

In the summer of 1944, the Red Army began **liberating** Poland. By July, the communist National Committee had set itself up at Lublin, the first major city to be freed.

In February 1945, at Yalta, the 'Big Three' agreed that the USA and Britain would accept the National Committee as the Polish government, provided that representatives of the London government were also included. In particular, they wanted the People's Party leader to be included. They also agreed that democratic Polish elections would be held that same year.

Just three months later, the communists took action. 16 nationalist (non-communist) **resistance** leaders were arrested and a new government was formed. It included the People's Party leader as Deputy Prime Minister.

B Propaganda on Polish stamps. The top one shows the world's workers meeting (1945). The lower one shows three communist members of the Committee of National Liberation (1946).

No elections were held in 1945. Instead, the country found itself practically fighting a civil war. Non-communist **partisans** fought a guerrilla war against communist security forces. A propaganda war was launched against the People's Party. By the summer of 1946, 1200 of their members had been arrested. And there were still no elections.

The elections finally took place in January 1947. By then, the communists had locked up about 100 000 members of the People's Party – as well as 142 election candidates.

At the election, communists frightened voters into voting for communist candidates. To no one's surprise, they won the election, winning 394 seats out of the 444. The 'free, democratic election' was over: the government which Stalin wanted had been elected.

The Iron Curtain

Two months later, Winston Churchill gave a speech in President Truman's home state, Missouri. He summed up his attitude towards the USSR and introduced a phrase which became famous – the 'Iron Curtain'.

> **C** Winston Churchill, speaking at Fulton in Missouri (March 1946):
>
> From Stettin in the Baltic to Trieste in the Adriatic, an iron curtain has descended across the continent. Behind that line lie all the capitals of the ancient states of central and eastern Europe. All these famous cities and the populations around them lie in the Soviet sphere and all are subject not only to Soviet influence but to a very high measure of control from Moscow.

Churchill wanted a new Anglo-American alliance against the USSR. In fact, Truman did not support this. Nor did most Americans want it. They still hoped that the USA and USSR would co-operate as they had during the war. But Churchill's speech made Stalin angry and, a week later, he replied.

D Winston Churchill giving his famous 'Iron Curtain' speech.

> **E** Joseph Stalin, quoted in *Pravda* (March 13 1946).
>
> There can be no doubt that Mr Churchill's position is a call for a war on the USSR.
>
> The Soviet Union's loss of life has been several times greater than that of Britain and the United States put together. The Soviet Union cannot forget them. And so what is surprising that the Soviet Union, anxious for its future safety, is trying to ensure that governments loyal to the Soviet Union should exist in these countries?

F This British cartoon had the title: 'A Peep Under the Iron Curtain' (1946).

> ### Q
>
> 1 a) Explain the steps by which the communists gained control of Poland up to 1946.
>   b) How did Stalin avoid a 'free' election being held in Poland?
> 2 a) What did Churchill mean by an 'iron curtain'?
>   b) Why are so many factories shown behind the iron curtain in source F?
> 3 a) Was Stalin justified in what he said in source E?
>   b) How do you think Stalin would have justified what happened in Poland?

The Communists Take Control

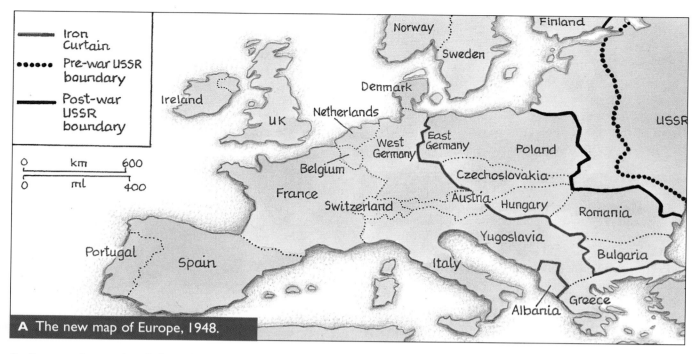

A The new map of Europe, 1948.

Stalin was determined that the USSR should not be invaded again. What he wanted was a 'buffer zone' of friendly countries between the USSR and Germany. The Second World War had made this possible.

The USSR had suffered much during the war. From 1941 to 1944, only the Soviet Red Army faced Germany on the mainland. By 1945, the Soviet Union had lost 20 million people.

From 1944 to April 1945, Soviet troops pushed German troops westwards across Europe. 'The Red Army was like a torrent of lava,' said a Soviet newspaper. By April 1945, it controlled almost all of eastern Europe. Soviet troops had reached Berlin itself. Stalin did not intend to give up the land which he had gained: this would be his buffer zone to protect the USSR.

Estonia, Latvia and Lithuania had became part of the USSR in 1940. At Yalta in 1945, the 'Big Three' had agreed that the USSR should keep part of Poland. Stalin also took land from Finland, Romania and Czechoslovakia. As a result, the USSR gained about 25 million people. More importantly, its border moved 300 miles west of where it had been in 1939.

Stalin had his buffer zone – but he wanted more than just friendly neighbours; he wanted communist ones. Naturally, local communists had welcomed Soviet troops. In return, Stalin gave local communist parties his support.

During 1944–5, a few important communists went home to their liberated countries. They had spent the war in Moscow, where they had been trained by the Soviet Communist Party. What happened next in countries freed by the Red Army followed a pattern. First, communists joined in a **coalition** government – but they took the key jobs, such as running the police and the army.

Next, the communists got rid of the opposition. Fascists and capitalists were tried or expelled. Evidence was found to cast doubt on non-communist politicians. Bit by bit, the opposition was whittled away.

Finally, an election was held when hardly any opponents were left. The candidates were all or mostly communists. When a communist government was elected, a 'people's democracy' was set up. Its key people were those same communists who had been trained in the Soviet Union.

For instance, the Red Army entered Hungary in September 1944. Free elections were held in November 1945 and they were won by the non-communist Smallholders' Party. In 1945–6, under Soviet pressure, secret police 'found evidence' against the Smallholders' Party and it lost power.

The United Workers' Party took over. Its leader was Mátyás Rákosi. He had been trained in Moscow during the war. Under his leadership, Hungary became a 'People's Republic' in 1949. It was given a new **constitution**, based on the Soviet Union's.

Rákosi described the whole process as 'like slicing off salami'. He meant to remove his opponents, one by one, until there was no opposition left.

Hungary was not alone. One by one, the countries bordering on the USSR became friendly communist neighbours. By March 1948, Stalin had also set up communist governments in Poland, East Germany, Romania, Bulgaria and Czechoslovakia. In each country, non-communist leaders had fled, been put in prison or were dead.

B Democracy in action: a Democratic Party gunman threatens the Romanian opposition in Bucharest.

But one resistance leader stood up to Stalin. He was Josip Broz, resistance leader in Yugoslovia. He was better known as 'Tito'. His partisan army played the main role in forcing the Germans out of the country. When war ended, he was already head of a new government. He was successful and popular: it meant he could stand up to Stalin.

A split was inevitable and it happened in 1948. Tito refused to accept Stalin's orders and Stalin accused him of being a traitor. Yugoslavia was expelled from the **Cominform**, a communist organisation controlled by Stalin. Stalin also cut off Soviet aid, hoping to force Tito to obey him. He failed: Yugoslavia became the only communist country that was independent of the USSR.

In 1943, the 'Big Three' had agreed that some eastern European countries could have governments friendly to the USSR after the war. And Stalin had warned Roosevelt that democracy in eastern Europe would not be the same as American democracy. This message did not at first sink in. 'People's democracies' were not what Roosevelt or Churchill had planned at Yalta.

Then, Churchill had been content to let Stalin have influence in Bulgaria, Romania and Hungary. However, the Red Army had advanced far faster than he had predicted or wanted. The Soviet 'empire' was greater than he had expected.

D Miroslav Mansfeld was a Czech who fought in the RAF during the war. Afterwards, he returned to Czechoslovakia. He described how it had changed (1991).

Before the war, you could speak openly in Czech against anything the Germans had done. [When] the Germans came, you couldn't speak. In 1946, after the election, you couldn't even speak to your friend about it. You just kept mum.

In 1945, people across the street would wave and greet you. After 1946, everybody just walked, didn't see anybody else. People were very frightened – they didn't know who was on the other side. There was just one year after the war when people could say what they liked to their oppressors. Then, a year later, it was 'Yes, master'.

E 1949: newly-communist countries celebrated Stalin's 70th birthday.

Q

1 a) Why was Stalin in a position to control eastern Europe?
   b) What could Truman have done about this at the Potsdam Conference? (Be realistic.)
   c) What could the people of eastern Europe have done to prevent it?
2 What evidence is there that Stalin's control of eastern Europe was planned well in advance? (More than one answer.)
3 'By 1945, it was inevitable that eastern Europe would become communist.' Do you think this is true? Explain your answer in detail.

At Yalta, the 'Big Three' had agreed that Britain would have influence in Greece and Stalin kept his word. In the Greek election of 1946, the communists were heavily defeated by royalists but the communists refused to give up.

They fought a guerrilla war against the Greek government and neighbouring communist countries sent help. Britain had 40 000 troops stationed in the country and gave money to the Greek government. She also gave money to the Turkish government which was under Soviet pressure.

By 1947, Britain could no longer afford this. In February, the British government told the USA that they would have to pull out of Greece and stop helping Turkey.

After the war, the USA had played little part in European affairs. American troops had stayed in Germany but the rest had been sent back to the States. In March 1947, President Truman completely changed this policy.

C A British cartoon of 1947.

A Truman told Congress on 12 March 1947:

> The United States has received from the Greek government an urgent appeal for financial and economic assistance. The very existence of the Greek State is today threatened by the terrorist activities of several thousand armed men, led by communists. The United States must supply this assistance.

B This Greek woman is telling an occupying army officer that she was forced to join the guerrillas.

So far, his speech was asking Congress for support just in Greece. But Truman went on to explain why the issue was so important:

D Truman asked for support against all communists.

> One way of life is based upon the will of the majority, and is distinguished by free institutions, representative government, free elections, guarantees of individual liberty, freedom of speech and religion, and freedom from political *oppression*.
>
> The second way of life is based upon the will of a minority forcibly imposed upon the majority. It relies upon terror and oppression, a controlled press and radio, fixed elections, and the suppression of personal freedoms.
>
> I believe that it must be the policy of the United States to support free peoples who are resisting attempted *subjugation* by armed minorities or by outside pressures.

Truman ended by asking for $400 million to help Greece and Turkey. Congress agreed. Less than three years later, the Greek communists gave up their struggle.

Truman had announced a major change in American policy. The idea that the USA should help countries defeat communism became known as the 'Truman Doctrine'. In effect, the USA was taking on the role of the world's policeman in an attempt to stop communism spreading. The new American policy was to contain communism. One of the ways of doing this would be to give help to poor countries because Truman believed that poor people were more likely to support the communists.

'The Cold War'

Just days after Truman's speech, the USSR and the western powers failed to reach an agreement over Germany. In April, a US special adviser, called Bernard Baruch, gave a speech in South Carolina. At the time, Congress was discussing the Truman Doctrine. Baruch described the new relationship between the USA and the USSR. For the first time in public, he spoke of a 'Cold War'.

That same year, President Truman set up the Central Intelligence Agency (CIA). Its job was to collect secret information and to undermine the USA's opponents. That meant the USSR, in particular.

The Marshall Plan

E A German poster advertising the Marshall Plan.

Events now moved fast. In June, General George Marshall, the new US Secretary of State, announced an ambitious plan. It would provide American money to help the countries of Europe to recover from the war. He believed Europe need-ed this money if it was to stand up to the USSR.

He also knew that the USA needed to trade with European countries. If Europe could not afford to buy American goods, American industry might go into a **recession.**

Britain's Foreign Secretary, Ernest Bevin, was enthusiastic. He told MPs: 'When the Marshall proposals were announced, I grabbed them with both hands. Europe can wait no longer.' Within days, Bevin was organising a European response to the plan.

Countries interested in the offer included Poland and Czechoslovakia. But, in July, the USSR condemned the plan. Soviet politicians claimed that the USA was using its money to put pressure on other countries.

Czechoslovakia agreed to attend talks until Stalin called the Czech Prime Minister to Moscow. Poland turned down the offer. So did Finland, which was afraid of upsetting the USSR.

Marshall toured Europe to find out how much money was needed and came up with the figure of $13 000 million. Truman asked Americans to go without meat on Tuesdays and eggs on Thursdays to help Europe. But the US Congress was doubt-ful: it argued about whether to give the aid.

Then, in February 1948, communists overthrew the government of Czechoslovakia. Truman persuaded Congress that the aid was essential to stop communist revolutions elsewhere in Europe. American politicians saw the threat and Congress agreed the money, after all.

The Marshall Plan was a big success. The aid came in the form of goods, loans or even gifts up to 1952. Food poured in; US machinery helped European factories to get back to normal; advisers helped to rebuild transport systems.

In western Europe, a European Recovery Programme (ERP) was set up; in 1948, this led to the Organisation for European Economic Co-operation (OEEC). In 1947, the USSR set up the Communist Information Bureau, better known as Cominform. In theory, this provided information to all communist parties. In fact, Stalin used it to keep communist **satellites** under his control.

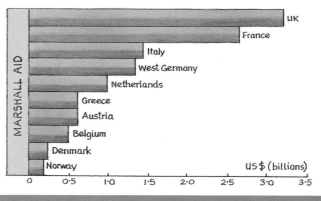

F How Marshall Plan aid was shared out.

> **Q**
>
> 1 a) What, exactly, was the Truman Doctrine?
>   b) Why did he introduce the idea?
>   c) How did the Marshall Plan help Europe?
>   d) How did the Marshall Plan help the USA?
> 2 Each side blamed the other for starting the Cold War. From what you have read, explain why (a) the USA should blame the USSR (b) why the USSR should blame the USA.

The Berlin Airlift

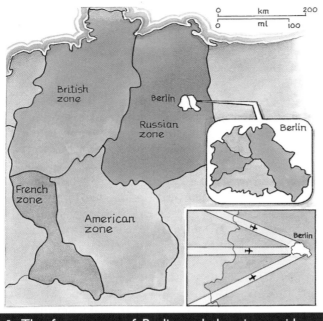

A The four zones of Berlin and the air corridors which connected Berlin with western Germany.

In 1945, Germany was divided into four zones and so was Berlin, its capital. The city was 100 miles inside the Russian zone of Germany; it was linked to the west by road, rail and air routes.

Stalin wanted Germany to stay weak and divided because a weak Germany was no threat to the USSR. Britain, France and the USA wanted Germany to be prosperous once more. While Germany remained poor, the Allies had to give food and money to the people. On the other hand, a wealthier Germany would be a stronger Germany: it could become western Europe's first line of defence against the USSR.

In the winter of 1947–8, the USA, USSR, France and Britain discussed the idea of introducing a new currency in Germany. However, the talks got nowhere because the USSR was totally against the idea. In June 1948, the western powers decided to go ahead anyway. A new currency called the Deutschmark was introduced into the three western zones.

It was not used in western Berlin in case this caused problems with the Russians – but problems came anyway. The USSR decided to introduce its own currency into East Germany, including East Berlin; the west retaliated by introducing the Deutschmark into western Berlin.

While these disagreements went on, the USSR decided to force the western Allies out of Berlin. In the middle of June, the main **autobahn** into West Berlin was closed for repairs. At 6.00 am on June 24, the USSR stopped all rail traffic between Berlin and western Germany.

West Berlin was surrounded by Soviet troops: the city was cut off. It was also short of power: gas, coal and electric supplies from East Berlin were stopped.

Two million people lived in West Berlin; unless the western powers helped them, they would starve within weeks. But what could the west do? General Clay, the governor of the American sector, wanted to send an armed convoy along the autobahn to force its way into Berlin. The Allies rejected the idea.

The airlift begins

However, there was one other possibility: the air routes were still open. Of course, the Russians might try to shoot down aeroplanes but the USA thought it was unlikely. After all, the USA had atom bombs – the USSR did not. So, on Saturday 26 June, the first planes landed at Templehof Airport in western Berlin. They carried a few tons of tinned food and mail.

It was more a gesture than anything else. The West Berliners needed a minimum of 5000 tons of food and other essential supplies every day. Existing food stocks were expected to last for just 36 days. The USSR did not think that an air-lift could supply everything that was needed. Even western reporters did not think an airlift would help the Berliners for long.

B Lieutenant Gail Halvorsen dropped thousands of sweets a day for Berlin children. The photograph shows him fitting them to parachutes made of handkerchiefs.

On July 2, the rescue operation got properly under way. The British codenamed it 'Operation Plainfare'. It was the start of the biggest air operation in history. Soon, planes were flying day and night along the air corridors. Each was given an exact time to land at 90-second intervals.

The pilots had a dangerous job: Soviet planes flew across the air corridors and weather balloons were placed in awkward positions. But Stalin always stopped short of closing the air corridors. He did not want to risk a war.

2000 hot water bottles

Ping-pong balls

Steamroller

Manhole covers

A goat for the Royal Welsh Fusiliers

Dog for a blind man

C The airlift brought more than food. These were some of the extras which were flown in.

By September, the planes were flying in 4600 tons of supplies a day – but it was still not enough. Meanwhile, the USSR tried to persuade the people of West Berlin to go and live in East Berlin. Less than three per cent of them took up the offer.

In West Berlin itself, civilians coped with the crisis. Food was rationed and each motorist was given just five gallons of petrol for a month. The subway trains and trams had stopped running.

The USSR hoped for a bad winter. Severe ice and snow would have limited flights; extreme cold would have killed the old and sick in the city. But the really bad weather never came. By January, Stalin knew his plan had failed.

The airlift ends

The airlift continued into the spring. It reached a peak on April 16–17 1949 when 1398 flights landed nearly 13 000 tons of supplies in 24 hours. By then, Stalin was seeking a way out. The USSR ended its blockade of West Berlin at midnight on May 12 1949. That evening, West Berliners put on evening dress and danced in the streets. They were waiting for the red and white pole to be lifted, allowing the first car through.

D This airlift memorial now stands at Templehof Airport, Berlin.

E This Soviet view of the airlift was given in *Soviet Foreign Policy* by Ilya Kremer (1968).

The Soviet military government was forced to take emergency measures to protect the life and currency of East Germany. Checks were made on travellers coming from West Germany in order to keep out *speculators* and profiteers. Some routes between Berlin and the western zones were cut.

The Soviet authorities were ready to provide food and fuel for the population of the whole of Berlin. However, the western occupying powers deprived the inhabitants of West Berlin of the possibility of obtaining any help from East Germany. The western powers claimed that there was a blockade of West Berlin by the Soviet Union.

The USA organised a so-called 'airlift' to supply West Berlin by air. This stunt served the purposes of propaganda. [It made] the 'Cold War' worse.

Q

1 Explain the events leading up to the Berlin Airlift.
2 a) What was the USSR trying to achieve?
   b) What were the western powers trying to achieve?
3 a) Compare source E with the text. How do they give different views of the airlift?
   b) Explain why they are different.
   c) What do they agree about?
4 Why might the Berlin Airlift make the Cold War worse?

RESULTS OF THE AIRLIFT

The Berlin Airlift may be seen as yet another event in the Cold War which had developed between the USSR and the USA. However, it was more than that. For the first time, the former Allies came close to fighting each other. The consequences of the airlift were enormous.

1 Germany was split

Any hope of reuniting Germany was now ended. In May 1949, the western Allies brought their zones together to form the Federal Republic of Germany, known as West Germany. In October, the eastern sector became a separate state, calling itself the German Democratic Republic (East Germany). It had become impossible to have a peace treaty with the whole of Germany – and there never was one.

Berlin, too, was more clearly divided than in the past. The British, Americans and French built up West Berlin to show the East Germans what capitalism could achieve. Meanwhile, the USSR encouraged East Berliners to think of themselves as part of East Germany.

A Clement Attlee, British PM from 1945-51, interviewed in 1960 (from *A Prime Minister Remembers*).

Questioner: What would you put as the turning point [of] American policy?
Attlee: The Berlin airlift. I think that was the decisive thing. It wasn't, I think, until the Berlin air-lift that American public opinion really wakened up to the facts of life. I don't think they really appreciated communist tactics until Berlin.

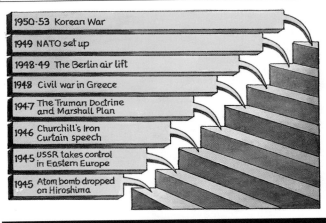

1950-53 Korean War
1949 NATO set up
1948-49 The Berlin air lift
1948 Civil war in Greece
1947 The Truman Doctrine and Marshall Plan
1946 Churchill's Iron Curtain speech
1945 USSR takes control in Eastern Europe
1945 Atom bomb dropped on Hiroshima

B Steps in the Cold War.

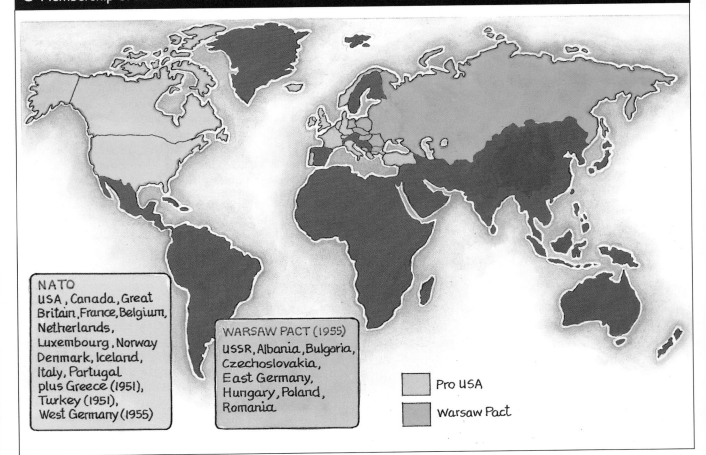

C Membership of NATO and the Warsaw Pact. Members of NATO joined in 1949, except where shown.

NATO
USA, Canada, Great Britain, France, Belgium, Netherlands, Luxembourg, Norway Denmark, Iceland, Italy, Portugal plus Greece (1951), Turkey (1951), West Germany (1955)

WARSAW PACT (1955)
USSR, Albania, Bulgaria, Czechoslovakia, East Germany, Hungary, Poland, Romania

Pro USA
Warsaw Pact

2 NATO and the Warsaw Pact

Even before the Berlin Airlift, some western countries had talked of setting up a defensive organisation to protect themselves from the USSR. In April 1949, 12 western nations signed a treaty setting up the North Atlantic Treaty Organisation (NATO). They agreed that, if one member was attacked, others would come to help them.

President Truman said it was 'a shield against aggression' but, at first, NATO was no match for the USSR if there had been a war. Four months after it was formed, the USSR exploded its first atomic bomb. By 1950, NATO had just 14 army divisions; the USSR and her allies could muster 173. NATO only developed as a major military force during the 1950s.

> **D** From the NATO Treaty (1949):
>
> **The Parties agree that an armed attack against one or more of them in Europe or North America shall be considered an attack against them all. Consequently they agree that, if such an armed attack occurs, each of them will assist the Party or Parties … by taking … such action as it deems necessary, including the use of armed force.**

The USSR condemned NATO. It said NATO was not defensive, but an offensive alliance against the USSR. It claimed that the west was preparing for war. Soviet opposition increased when Turkey and Greece joined NATO in 1951.

Source C shows that the USSR had every reason to be nervous: it was almost surrounded by NATO members. There were new Soviet complaints when West Germany joined NATO in 1955. The USSR replied by setting up its own organisation, called the Warsaw Pact. This tied eastern Europe (except for Yugoslavia) closer to the USSR.

Each member of the Pact agreed to help any other member which was attacked. They agreed that Soviet troops should stay in four member countries and a Soviet general took command of the Warsaw Pact forces. The Pact's HQ was in Moscow. Much of the world was now divided into two armed camps.

3 The arms race

The conflict over Berlin was the only occasion when the superpowers confronted each other in Europe. But, from 1949 onwards, there was no trust between the USSR and the USA. Each side felt threatened; as a result, each side made alliances and each side built more weapons.

And the result? Each side felt even more threatened. During the 1950s, the US army increased to 3.5 million men while its air force doubled. The Soviet Union had even greater forces.

> **E** Milestones in the arms race.
>
> | | |
> |---|---|
> | 1945 | USA – A-BOMB |
> | 1949 | RUSSIA – A-BOMB |
> | 1952 | BRITAIN – A-BOMB |
> | 1952 | USA – H-BOMB |
> | 1953 | USSR – H-BOMB |
> | 1957 | BRITAIN – H-BOMB |
> | 1957 | USSR – INTERCONTINENTAL BALLISTIC MISSILE (ICBM) |
> | 1960 | FRANCE – A-BOMB |

One thing made this arms race more dangerous than any other arms race in history: nuclear weapons. Any country with atom bombs had the power to destroy any other country on earth. In 1945, only the USA had them. Once the USSR built its own, an arms race began.

It was not just that the superpowers were developing new bombs; they were also building bigger bombs. A single hydrogen bomb could destroy an entire city. By the mid-1950s, American B52 bombers, based in Europe, could have wiped out Moscow. The USSR was behind the USA in nuclear development but it could still have destroyed its rival.

In the 1960s, the US President boasted that the USA had enough missiles to wipe out the USSR twice.

> Q
>
> 1 a) Put these events in chronological order: NATO set up; the German Democratic Republic created; the Berlin Airlift; the Warsaw Pact created; the Federal Republic of Germany created.
>   b) How are these events linked up?
> 2 a) What were the short-term consequences of the Soviet blockade of Berlin?
>   b) What were the long-term consequences?
> 3 a) What did the West claim was the purpose of NATO?
>   b) Why should Stalin not believe this?

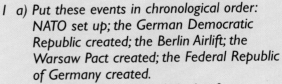

War in Korea 1950–53

The lead up to war

In 1949, the communists took control in China. This was a blow to the USA because Americans had been supporting Chinese Nationalists. It seemed as though the American policy of containing communism had failed in Asia. One year later, attention was focussed on China's neighbour, Korea.

Korea had been ruled by Japan until Japan was defeated in 1945. At Yalta, Britain, the USA and USSR had agreed that Soviet and American troops should occupy Korea when the war ended. The country was divided along the 38th parallel, until a democratic government could be elected to rule the whole country. Soviet troops moved into northern Korea and American troops moved into the southern part.

The UN tried to have elections but the USSR rejected the idea. In August 1948, the Americans set up a republic in the south (the Republic of Korea); Syngman Rhee became its first president. A month later, the Russians set up a communist republic in the north (the Korean People's Democratic Republic). It was ruled by Kim Il Sung, a Red Army captain. Each claimed to represent the whole of Korea.

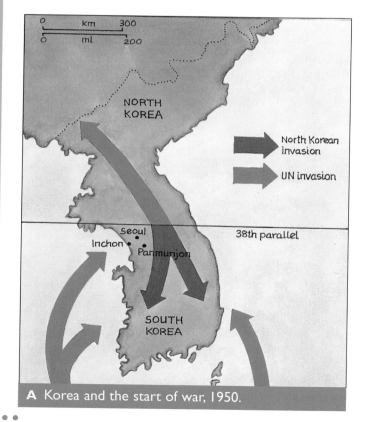

A Korea and the start of war, 1950.

The United Nations reckoned that 18000 people died on the border during the next two years of 'peace'. After the USA and USSR withdrew their troops, the two Korean governments went on arguing.

At dawn on June 25 1950, these arguments led to war when North Korean troops launched a huge surprise attack on the south. The army had been equipped and trained by the USSR. Within three days, it had captured South Korea's capital, Seoul.

B A British cartoon at the start of the war.

The UN is involved

The Americans acted quickly. President Truman sent supplies to the South Koreans and battleships to wait off the coast. He also asked the UN Security Council to take action. This was the first major test for the United Nations which had been formed only five years earlier. Would it take action?

When the Security Council met to discuss Korea, the USSR's representative was absent. The USSR had walked out of the UN as a protest because communist China was excluded. The Soviet Union would probably have used its **veto** to stop UN involvement – but it was not there to do so.

The Security Council passed a **resolution**, asking North Korea to leave South Korea. The North Koreans ignored this. So, days later, it passed a second resolution. This one asked UN members to send troops to help South Korea.

About 20 of the UN's 60 members eventually provided men and equipment but it was mainly an American force. About half of the soldiers were American and the USA provided nearly all of the navy and air force. The force was led by an American, General Douglas MacArthur. He took his orders from the American president, not from the UN.

By August 1950, North Korean troops occupied nearly all of South Korea. In September, American and South Korean troops landed at Inchon, 200 miles behind the North Korean front line. The North Koreans realised they might be surrounded and quickly retreated.

However, the Americans did not stop when they had pushed the North Koreans back to the 38th parallel. General MacArthur, leading the UN troops, invaded North Korea and by October had reached the Yalu River on the Chinese frontier. This worried the Chinese who were afraid that their new communist state would be attacked.

China joins in

Before the war began, a number of countries had recognised the new People's Republic of China. This meant that they accepted that it was an independent nation. They included Britain. However, the USA refused to recognise communist China so the Chinese were wary of the Americans.

At first, the Chinese were worried that the USA might use atomic bombs against them. But western spies told Chinese leaders that President Truman would not agree to use them. So, when the USA ignored Chinese warnings, the Chinese launched a surprise attack across the Korean border.

C A portrait photograph of Kim Il Sung.

Who caused the Korean War?

D Nikita Khrushchev (later Soviet leader): *Khrushchev Remembers* (1971).

At the end of 1949, Kim Il Sung arrived to hold consultations with Stalin. The North Koreans wanted to prod South Korea with the point of a bayonet. Kim Il Sung said that the first poke would touch off an explosion in South Korea and that [they would turn communist].

Stalin persuaded Kim Il Sung that he should think it over, make some calculations, and then come back with a concrete plan. Kim went home and then returned to Moscow when he had worked everything out. He told Stalin he was certain of success. I remember Stalin had his doubts. He was worried that the Americans would jump in but we were inclined to think that if the war were fought swiftly, then intervention by the USA could be avoided.

Nevertheless, Stalin decided to ask Mao Tse-tung's opinion. [Mao Tse-Tung was the Chinese leader.] I must stress that the war wasn't Stalin's idea, but Kim Il Sung's. Stalin, of course, didn't try to [stop] him.

E Senior KGB officer, speaking in 1995:

Stalin had complete control. Every single action of Kim Il Sung was controlled by Soviet agents.

F Li Sang Cho was the chief North Korean army leader at the time. In 1990, he told *Moscow News*:

Kim Il Sung was the mastermind behind the war and he consulted Stalin about it. He did his best to convince Stalin of the plan's guaranteed success. [He] received Stalin's go-ahead, despite Stalin's concern about Washington getting involved.

Q

1 How did these events affect the Korean War:
  a) the communists gaining power in China;
  b) the USSR walking out of the UN;
  c) the USA having atomic bombs?
2 a) Which side did the USA support and how did it help them?
  b) Which side did the USSR support and how did it help them?
  c) Look at the situation at the end of 1950. Why was it dangerous?

THE END OF THE WAR

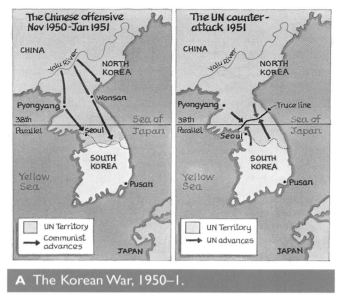

A The Korean War, 1950–1.

The USA ignored Chinese warnings. Late in 1950, Chinese troops arrived to help the North Koreans. The Chinese army numbered 180 000 men, with another 100 000 in reserve: it was too big for the UN force to cope with. They were 'just like a crowd at a football match,' according to a UN pilot. Within a fortnight, UN troops were pushed back into South Korea.

The UN force managed to halt the Chinese advance in late January. Two months later, the Chinese were pushed back across the 38th parallel into North Korea. MacArthur wanted to attack China itself. Many Americans wanted President Truman to use atomic bombs against the Chinese but he refused. MacArthur was sacked when he, too, advised the use of atom bombs.

For nearly a year, the war had see-sawed back and forth across Korea. Now, it settled into a stalemate. The two sides dug trenches and faced each other across the 38th parallel. But the fighting went on. Peace talks were held at Panmunjom but dragged on for two years. While the USA and China argued, the death toll rose.

In November 1952, General Eisenhower was elected as the new US President after promising to end the Korean War. He also threatened to bomb the Chinese with America's new hydrogen bomb. Then, in March 1953, Stalin died and the USSR stopped supplying weapons to the Chinese.

Soon afterwards, the Chinese agreed to talks and an **armistice** was signed at Panmunjom on July 27 1953. The two sides agreed to fix the border close to the 38th parallel, where it had been before the war started.

The war's results

It was a costly war. As many as four million people may have died. They included 54 000 Americans and about 7000 from the British Commonwealth. Whole areas of Korea had been destroyed; they included millions of homes.

The war led to an increase in the arms race. The USA developed a hydrogen bomb in 1952; a year later, the USSR tested one. In the 1960s, the Chinese developed both atomic and hydrogen bombs.

The war had been a testing-ground for other weapons. US troops used flame-throwers to destroy undergrowth in which enemy troops could hide. US planes dropped napalm: it burns trees and bushes easily; it also sticks to human beings and burns their flesh. Both these weapons would be used again in the Vietnam War.

It was an important war for the United Nations. The League of Nations had failed to stop aggression in the 1930s. The UN had proved that it could raise an army and that it was prepared to stand up to aggression. Without the UN action, it is unlikely that South Korea would still exist.

In August 1950, the USSR again took its seat in the Security Council to make sure the UN could not take more steps without its agreement. It was soon using its veto again. But Stalin blamed the UN Secretary General, Trygve Lie, for getting the UN involved in Korea. Soviet representatives at the UN refused to work with him, which made his position almost impossible. In 1953, he resigned.

But the UN failed to bring democracy to Korea. Kim ruled the north as a **dictator** until his death in 1994. Syngman Rhee was forced out of office in 1960 after complaints about government corruption. Neither North nor South has had a good record on human rights.

B This Soviet cartoon accused Trygve Lie of allowing UN troops to use germ warfare in Korea (1952).

Above all, the UN failed to unite Korea. The border remains on the 38th parallel and all efforts to unite the country have failed. Both North and South still claim the right to rule the whole of Korea.

C British Field-Marshal Alanbrooke met General MacArthur in November 1945. These were the general's views (from *Triumph in the West*, 1959).

> In his opinion we should be prepared for trouble and assemble at least a thousand atomic bombs in England and in the States. With a combined attack from east and west, Russia could be brought to her senses if she started giving trouble.

D One of the thousands of refugees. Everything he owns is on his back.

E Alexander Orlov worked with Soviet military intelligence during the Korean War. In 1995, he said:

> All our military wore Chinese uniforms without badges of rank. Advisers in Korea wore civilian clothes. All contact was forbidden between Soviet military and American POWs [prisoners-of-war].

F President Truman considered a direct attack on the USSR. He wrote in his diary in January 1952:

> It seems to me that the proper approach now would be an *ultimatum* [to] Moscow. This means all-out war. Every manufacturing plant in China and the Soviet Union will be eliminated. This is the final chance for the Soviet government to decide whether it wishes to survive or not.

Was World War III a real risk?

It had been a very dangerous war indeed. During the war, the USSR had an airforce division based in northern China and support troops in North Korea. These included radar units and anti-aircraft guns. They were all used to fight American troops.

From 1951–3, American and Soviet planes fought each other over Korea. Soviet pilots wore Chinese uniforms and put Chinese symbols on their planes. In effect, Stalin had ordered Soviet troops to fight American ones. American leaders knew what was happening but kept it secret. If the American people had learned about it, they would have wanted a direct attack on the USSR.

The USA and Britain were both worried that the USSR might test the western powers elsewhere. Western leaders believed that there was a greater risk of a world war because of Korea. The war convinced the west that Stalin would do anything to expand Soviet power.

They had good reason to be concerned. Stalin had greater control over the war than western intelligence knew at the time. At one point, Stalin even considered whether to use Soviet troops to attack UN troops in Korea.

> The Chinese took 3000 Americans as prisoners-of-war. After the Korean War, 21 chose to stay in Communist China.

G Stalin considered war with the USA. He sent this telegram to Mao Zedong in October 1950.

> Should we fear this? I think not, because together we shall be stronger than America, England and the other capitalist states. Without Germany, they do not represent a serious military power. If war is inevitable, then let it be now.

H Mao Zedong replied in October 1950.

> I am very happy that in your reply the joint struggle of the USSR and China against the Americans is discussed. Undoubtedly, if we are to fight, then we should fight now.

Q

> 1 Read source C. Was MacArthur a good choice as UN commander? Give reasons.
> 2 Was the UN really involved in the Korean War or was it America's war? Explain your answer fully.
> 3 How close do you think World War III really was? Use the sources in your answer.

In the early 1950s, many Americans believed that the USSR was trying to turn the whole world communist. This was what President Truman himself believed. So did President Eisenhower, who took over from him in 1953. As a result, Eisenhower built up American armed forces and nuclear weapons. He also followed Truman's policy of containment – trying to contain communism and stop it spreading.

One way of achieving this was to build up a series of alliances. NATO was the first in 1949. It was followed by **SEATO** (South East Asia Treaty Organisation) in 1954. The USA, Britain and France allied with five eastern countries. They agreed to act jointly if one of them were attacked. In 1955, the Baghdad Pact linked up five nations with the USA.

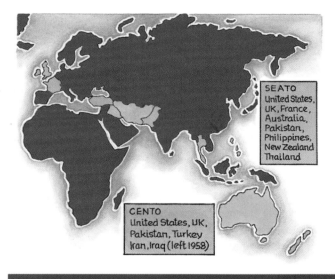

SEATO
United States, UK, France, Australia, Pakistan, Philippines, New Zealand Thailand

CENTO
United States, UK, Pakistan, Turkey Iran, Iraq (left 1958)

A SEATO and the Baghdad Pact, later known as CENTO (the Central Treaty Organisation).

After Stalin

Stalin died in 1953 and the Cold War thawed a little. After a power struggle, Nikita Khrushchev emerged as the new Soviet leader. In 1955, he met western leaders at a summit meeting in Geneva. They agreed that Austria should now become an independent state. (They had jointly occupied it since 1945.)

In the following year, Khrushchev called for 'peaceful co-existence' with the USA. What he meant was that the two superpowers would have to learn to live peacefully with each other.

> Khrushchev, 1955:
>
> **'Stalin was a god; he could make and unmake men and things; we can't.'**

The Twentieth Party Congress (1956)

In February 1956, Khrushchev made a secret speech at the Twentieth Party Congress in Moscow. He attacked Stalin, blaming him for much that had happened in the USSR before the war. Khrushchev told senior party officials that Stalin had been a ruthless, brutal dictator.

Most of the major communist leaders in eastern Europe owed their jobs to Stalin's support. People in these countries angrily discussed the 'secret' speech and attacked **Stalinist** leaders. In June 1956, there were strikes and riots at Poznan in Poland: 53 workers were killed. A popular leader, Gomulka, was brought back to carry out reforms.

In Hungary, it was far worse – there was open revolt. The Hungarians had resented Soviet control of their country ever since it became communist in 1948. Hungary was a religious nation but its Catholic schools had been **nationalised** and religion was frowned upon. Schoolchildren were forced to learn communist history. In addition, the secret police (the AVO) were feared and Soviet troops still remained in the country.

Khrushchev's speech made the Hungarians feel they now had a chance to get rid of their own Stalinist leaders. At first, they were successful. The USSR forced the local communist leader, Rákosi, to resign in July. But the Hungarians were still dissatisfied: the harvest was poor and fuel was in short supply.

B The Budapest statue of Stalin was destroyed (see next page).

C The *Daily Mail* gave news of Soviet tanks moving into Hungary, 5 November 1956.

The Hungarian Uprising (1956)

On October 23, students and workers in the capital Budapest held a demonstration. The Communist Party leader rejected their demands and police fired into the crowd. What had begun peacefully quickly turned into a rebellion.

A huge statue of Stalin was pulled down and dragged round the streets on a rubbish cart. Secret police were lynched and communist leaders were hanged from the trees. To calm things down, Soviet troops being withdrawing from Hungary and a moderate communist, called Imre Nagy, came to power. (You pronounce it: Nodj.)

Nagy brought non-communists into his government and released a leading Catholic called Cardinal Mindszenty. But the situation was going beyond Nagy's control. Communists and anti-communists had joined forces. Communists wanted to end Stalinist rule; anti-communists wanted to get rid of the communists altogether. The Communist Party itself began to fall apart. Its newspaper was not published.

On October 30, Nagy accepted all the rebels' demands. On the following day, he asked the USSR to take its troops out of Hungary. On November 1, he announced that Hungary would leave the Warsaw Pact and become **neutral**. He appealed to the United Nations and asked for western help in defending the country.

Khrushchev could not tolerate this. On November 4, Soviet tanks moved into Budapest to put down the uprising. The Hungarian people fought back with home-made weapons, such as petrol bombs, but it was a one-sided fight.

About 20 000 Hungarians were killed and another 150 000 fled abroad. Nagy took refuge in the Yugoslav Embassy. Later in November, he was tricked out and arrested. He was executed in 1958.

Cardinal Mindszenty spent the next 15 years hiding in the US Embassy before he was allowed to leave Hungary.

Nagy was replaced by the pro-Soviet Janos Kádár. He later carried out many of the reforms which Nagy had suggested but Hungary did not leave the Warsaw Pact. Nor did it become neutral.

Khrushchev's process of de-Stalinisation went slower after 1956 but he had shown that, in one respect, he differed little from Stalin. He had shown that eastern Europe was firmly under Soviet control and was going to stay that way.

> **D** Radio Kossuth, 24 October 1956.
>
> **Fascist reactionary elements have started an armed attack against our public buildings and have also attacked our police. In the interest of restoring order, and until further notice is given, we announce that it is forbidden to hold any meetings, rallies and parades.**

> **E** Hungarian news report, 4 November 1956.
>
> **People are jumping up at the tanks, throwing hand grenades inside and then slamming the driver's windows. The Hungarian people are not afraid of death. It is only a pity that we can't stand for long.**

Q

1. a) What were the long-term and short-term causes of the Hungarian uprising?
   b) What were its results?
2. a) Read sources C, D and E. Which side was each writer on? Explain how you decided.
   b) Are these sources propaganda? Explain your decisions.

PEACEFUL CO-EXISTENCE

A Khrushchev said in 1959:

There are only two ways: either peaceful coexistence or the most destructive war in history. There is no third way.

There were good reasons for following this policy. By 1960, each superpower already had enough nuclear weapons to destroy the other. Neither side gained anything by increasing tension. There was a risk it might lead to a nuclear war which nobody wanted. Also, if the USA and USSR could agree on arms cuts, it would save money.

Yet the build-up of arms went on. In 1953, the USSR successfully tested its own H-bomb. In 1957, it produced an intercontinental ballistic missile (**ICBM**), just months before the USA produced its own ICBM. That same year, the USSR launched the first space satellite, **Sputnik** 1.

Another summit meeting was planned for May 1960 but, on 1 May, the Russians shot down an American plane which had been flying over the USSR. It was a U-2 spy plane, designed to take photographs of Soviet military targets. These flights had been going on for three years. When President Eisenhower refused to apologise, the meeting collapsed. It had lasted just three hours. Overhead, a Soviet sputnik circled the globe twice.

B Nikita Khrushchev, quoted in *Overkill: The Story of Modern Weapons* by J Cox (1981).

President Kennedy once stated that the United States had the [missiles] to wipe out the Soviet Union two times over, while the Soviet Union had enough atomic weapons to wipe out the United States only once. Journalists asked me to comment. I said jokingly, 'He's quite right. But I'm not complaining. Once is quite enough. What good does it do to [destroy] a country twice? We're not a bloodthirsty people.'

The arms race continued into the 1960s as each superpower built more nuclear weapons and developed new ones. In 1963, both the USA and the USSR produced their first nuclear submarines.

One key reason for this was money. Nuclear missiles were cheaper to make than many conventional weapons. Also, having nuclear weapons meant that the USA did not need a large army. It seemed as if building nuclear weapons saved money but ordinary people in many nations were frightened of them.

The word 'summit' to describe top-level talks became common after Churchill used it in 1950.

In 1994, Britain revealed that the RAF had carried out secret spy flights for the USA in 1952 and 1954. RAF crews had flown American plans, repainted in RAF colours, over the Soviet Union. Presidents Truman and Eisenhower had banned the USAF from making its own flights.

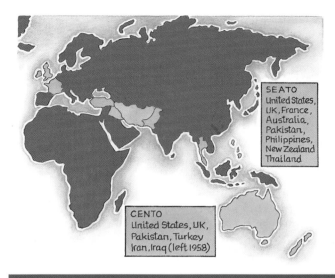

SEATO
United States, UK, France, Australia, Pakistan, Philippines, New Zealand, Thailand

CENTO
United States, UK, Pakistan, Turkey, Iran, Iraq (left 1958)

C A British cartoon of the 1960s.

East Berlin

After the Hungarian Revolution of 1956, the USSR faced less open opposition in Europe, although many eastern Europeans did not want to live behind the Iron Curtain. However, there was one place where they could leave and that was through East Berlin.

East Berlin was a problem for the USSR. In 1953, building workers had gone on strike when the communist government increased the work they had to do by 10 per cent. As the strike spread, people demonstrated not only against their communist government but also against the USSR.

These demonstrations spread to East Germany and the police could not control them. After two days, Soviet tanks moved onto the streets of Berlin and ended the disturbances. Crowds shouted, 'Ivan, go home'.

The revolt was over but the problem of East Berlin did not go away. It was the one place in eastern Europe where people in communist countries had easy contact with people in the West. East Berliners could see the living standards of West Berliners; they could see what was on sale in the shops – and they were jealous.

Ever since the Berlin Airlift, people had been leaving East Germany to live in the west. The total East German population was about 20 million; from 1949 onwards, over two thousand of them were leaving every day.

Communist soldiers patrolled the border between East and West Germany to stop people leaving. However, in Berlin, it was easy to get to the West. Every day, Berliners crossed the city to go to work or visit relatives. Many simply never returned.

Khrushchev wanted to solve this problem with a German peace treaty. In 1958, he demanded that all foreign troops should be pulled out of Berlin. The west believed this was part of a plan to make West Berlin part of East Germany – and therefore communist. They refused to agree.

Meanwhile, in Berlin, the refugees increased. In 1960, 199 000 East Germans left their country to live in the West. In the first six months of 1961, another 103 000 left. In August, over 3000 refugees a day were reaching West Berlin.

It was bad for communist propaganda that so many people seemed to prefer capitalism to communism. Even worse, East Germany could not afford to lose all these people, especially as many of them were skilled workers.

Khrushchev had hoped to reach an agreement over Berlin at the 1960 summit meeting. When talks collapsed, the USSR looked for a different solution to the problem of East Berlin.

D 'See how many are staying on our side'.

The Berlin Wall (1961)

Just after midnight on August 13 1961, the East German government took action. Police sealed off most of the crossing points in Berlin with barbed wire. On August 17, communist troops began to build a wall of concrete blocks. Anyone trying to escape was shot. Four died within two months.

Western leaders protested but there was little they could do. Extra American troops and British tanks were sent to West Berlin – but the wall stayed. To the outside world, it looked as if the USSR had won.

E This East Berlin frontier guard leaps to freedom in West Berlin, August 1961.

Churchill's 'Iron Curtain' had become real. In later years, West Berlin became a symbol of communist oppression. President Kennedy visited it in 1963.

F President Kennedy told West Berliners:

There are many people in the world who really don't understand what is the great issue between the free world and the communist world.

Let them come to Berlin!

There are some who say in Europe and elsewhere we can work with the communists.

Let them come to Berlin!

All free men, wherever they may live, are citizens of Berlin. Therefore, as a free man, I take pride in the words 'Ich bin ein Berliner' [I am a Berliner].

The West Berlin crowd went wild. On the other side of the wall, East Germans cheered and someone threw a bouquet over the wall.

Q

1 a) Why did Britain keep the spy flights secret at the time?
   b) What does this teach you about the problems of studying recent history?
2 a) Why was Berlin a problem for the USSR?
   b) How did the Berlin Wall help to solve that problem?
   c) Why do you think the west didn't use force to tear the Wall down?

7

The Cuban Missiles Crisis (1962)

By 1960, the two superpowers had enough nuclear missiles to wipe out each other and everyone else as well. However, they were still nervous. What would happen if their missiles were destroyed before they could use them? Or suppose they were destroyed in mid-flight? Both the USA and USSR became worried that nuclear missiles did not offer a final solution.

So each side developed its own **nuclear deterrents**. These would deter the enemy from using its missiles. This would be achieved by making sure that your own side could still strike back even after being attacked by nuclear weapons. This would result in both sides being wiped out.

A 'The important thing is not winning... but taking part'. This 1960 cartoon shows different leaders in the nuclear arms race.

Background

The island of Cuba lies about 90 miles off the United States coast. From 1952 to 1959, it was ruled by a dictator called General Batista. The USA supported him for most of that time. American companies controlled much of Cuban business. As long as Cuba was at peace, American business profited. So the USA supplied Batista with arms.

However, Batista's rule became more and more brutal and, in 1957, the USA cut off the arms supplies. It wanted a more effective government so it encouraged a resistance movement, led by Fidel Castro. In 1959, he overthrew Batista's government and became Cuban President. By then, he had become communist.

The friendly relations between Castro and the USA did not last for long. Castro began a series of reforms, which included nationalising some industries. Many of these were American.

Also, Castro blamed the USA for the island's poverty and sought aid from the USSR. When the USA refused to buy Cuba's sugar, the USSR agreed to take the sugar in return for the oil and machinery.

The Bay of Pigs (1961)

President Eisenhower promised to help Cuban refugees who wanted to get rid of Castro. In January 1961, John F Kennedy took over as US President, the youngest in the country's history. He was told of a CIA plan to invade Cuba and overthrow Castro. He allowed the plan to go ahead and the result was a disaster.

On April 17, about 1500 of Castro's opponents landed at Cochinos Bay ('the Bay of Pigs') on the southern coast of Cuba. They were equipped with arms provided by the USA. These rebels had told the CIA that the Cubans would join them and overthrow Castro; they did not.

The group was badly trained and poorly armed and equipped. Even their maps were out-of-date. In any case, they were outnumbered by almost 300 to one. Within three days, the invaders were either dead or in prison.

The results of this invasion were the opposite to what the CIA intended. First, the Cuban army had defeated the invaders so easily that Castro became more popular. Secondly, Castro now saw the USA as a very serious threat indeed. He asked Khrushchev for help to defend Cuba.

B This invader was captured two days later.

C This was what Kennedy told a friend after the Bay of Pigs failure (from *Kennedy* by R Gadney, 1983).

How could I have been so far off base? All my life I've known better than to depend on the experts. How could I have been so stupid to let them go ahead?

What should Kennedy do?

Kennedy faced a difficult decision. The Cold War was at its height and the USSR seemed to be winning it. In 1960, the USA had been publicly humiliated when a U-2 spy plane had been shot down over the Soviet Union. In August 1961, the communists had built the Berlin Wall (see page 21).

The USA had been embarrassed again in 1961 when the world learned of the Bay of Pigs fiasco. Was Khrushchev testing Kennedy's nerve, to see whether the young president would stand up to him? Whether he was or not, Kennedy had to decide what to do about the Cuban missiles.

'This is the week I had better earn my salary' – John F Kennedy, October 18 1962

E This American photo showed Soviet missiles heading for Cuba (1962).

Missile sites

Throughout 1962, American intelligence kept watch over Cuba. In the summer, CIA agents reported that Soviet ships were seen heading for the island. Down at the docks, Cubans were thrown out of their homes while Soviet sentries guarded ships which were being unloaded.

In September, the USSR admitted supplying arms to Castro but said they were for Cuban defence only. This seemed to make sense: if the USSR wished to attack the USA with nuclear weapons, it did not need to go to Cuba to do it. It could have launched them from bases within the USSR.

But CIA agents sent in different reports. Cuban exiles told them of convoys of lorries, carrying large objects, covered by tarpaulins. Others claimed that they had seen missiles being set up.

On 16 October 1962, Kennedy received evidence which suggested that Khrushchev had lied. An American U-2 spy plane had flown over Cuba and taken photographs. They showed that rocket-launching sites were being built on the island. From these sites the Cubans would be able to fire atomic missiles at almost any major American city.

> **F** These six options were considered by Kennedy's advisers (adapted from *Kennedy* by T C Sorensen, 1965.):
>
> 1 **Do nothing.**
> 2 **Put pressure on the USSR, perhaps through the United Nations. Another idea was to offer to remove US missile bases in Turkey in exchange for the removal of Cuban missiles.**
> 3 **Approach Castro secretly, to break off his Soviet links.**
> 4 **Blockade Cuba, e.g. by putting ships around it.**
> 5 **Launch an air attack.**
> 6 **Invade Cuba.**

Q

> 1 Read source F.
>   a) Take each action in turn. What risks would Kennedy be taking?
>   b) Decide what you would have done and present your ideas to the class.

KENNEDY'S DECISION

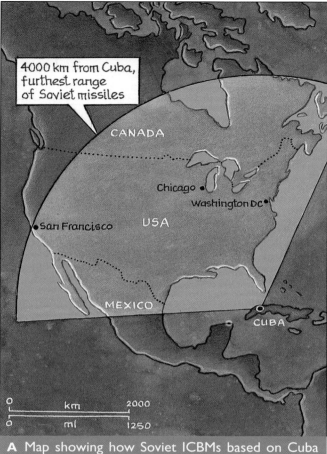

4000 km from Cuba, furthest range of Soviet missiles

CANADA

Chicago •
Washington DC •

• San Francisco

USA

MEXICO

CUBA

| km | 2000 |
| ml | 1250 |

A Map showing how Soviet ICBMs based on Cuba could have wiped out much of the United States.

Kennedy consulted with his advisers and decided to use the US navy to blockade Cuba. This would stop Soviet ships from landing any more missiles or other weapons. However, there was no guarantee that the USSR would tolerate this. They might take action themselves, such as seizing West Berlin.

So, in western America, 156 ICBMs were primed, ready to be fired at once. Meanwhile, the US air force was put on stand-by and nuclear bombs were loaded into the bomb bays.

The outside world knew nothing of this. The first news of the crisis was given by President Kennedy himself when he appeared on television on October 22. He announced the blockade and asked Khrushchev to stop supplying missiles to Cuba. And he went further:

B From Kennedy's TV speech, October 22 1962:

It shall be the policy of this nation to regard any nuclear missile launched from Cuba against any nation in the Western Hemisphere as an attack by the Soviet Union on the United States, requiring a full *retaliatory* response upon the Soviet Union.

The Soviet decision

Kennedy's meaning was obvious. If a Cuban missile was launched, the USA would attack the USSR. The world held its breath. On 23 October, the Soviet Press Officer at the UN told an American: 'This could well be our last conversation. New York will be blown up tomorrow by Soviet nuclear weapons. The Kremlin won't stand for this!'

Some American children were sent to school with rations and extra clothes, in case they had to go to public shelters.

In fact, he was wrong. The following day, 12 Soviet ships heading for Cuba either stopped or changed course. 'We're eyeball to eyeball,' said the US Secretary of State, 'and I think the other fellow just blinked.'

On Cuba itself, work continued on the missile sites. In the United States, Kennedy **mobilised** troops, ready for a possible invasion of Cuba. But the Russians were looking for a way out of the crisis. The two leaders talked by telephone and Khrushchev sent Kennedy two letters.

C This is from Khrushchev's first letter, received on 26 October 1962.

This is my proposal. No more weapons to Cuba and those within Cuba withdrawn or destroyed, and you respond by ending your blockade and also agree not to invade Cuba. Do not interfere with Russian ships.

D Around the world, there were demonstrations against American policy on Cuba. This one was in London.

> Your rockets are situated in Britain, situated in Italy and are aimed at us. Your rockets are situated in Turkey. You are worried by Cuba. You say that it worries you because it is a distance of 90 miles from America, but Turkey is next to us. Our sentries walk up and down and look at each other.
>
> I therefore make this proposal: we agree to remove [the missiles] from Cuba; we agree to carry this out and make a pledge to the United Nations. Your representatives will [declare] that the United States will remove its [missiles] from Turkey.

How did it end?

Many people believed that a nuclear war might start at any minute. On one occasion, the US navy boarded a USSR merchant ship – but the USSR did not retaliate. On another occasion, a Soviet missile shot down a U-2 plane over Cuba: this time, the USA took no action.

The crisis ended on October 28. The public was told that the USSR agreed to remove its missiles from Cuba and not install any more. In return, Kennedy ended the American blockade and promised not to invade the island.

In fact, President Kennedy had struck a secret deal with the USSR. Neither the public nor the US government was told about it. Kennedy had promised to remove some missiles from Europe if Khrushchev removed Soviet ones from Cuba. In November 1962, the Soviet missiles were dismantled. In April 1963, American Jupiter missiles were quietly withdrawn from Britain, Italy and Turkey.

Results of the crisis

The two superpowers had come dangerously close to a war. Neither Kennedy nor Khrushchev wanted to run the risk of a similar clash in the future. So a direct telephone line was set up in 1963 between Moscow and Washington. The two leaders could use this 'hotline' to talk directly to each other at just a few minutes' notice.

In that same year, a Test Ban Treaty was signed by the USA, USSR and Britain. They agreed to stop all nuclear tests in the atmosphere. However, it was not signed by either France or China. The French already had an atomic bomb; China exploded its first in 1964.

G Nikita Khrushchev gave his view of the crisis in his autobiography, *Khrushchev Remembers* (1971).

> We had to find a way of stopping American interference in the Caribbean. The answer was missiles. I had the idea of installing missiles with nuclear warheads in Cuba without letting the United States find out they were there until it was too late to do anything about them. We had no desire to start a war.
>
> We sent the Americans a note saying that we agreed to remove our missiles and bombers on the condition that the President [promised] that there would be no invasion of Cuba by the forces of the United States or anybody else.
>
> Finally Kennedy gave in and agreed to [give] us such an assurance. It was a great victory for us, a spectacular success without having to fire a single shot!

H President Kennedy gave his opinion in a private conversation, quoted in *A Thousand Days* (1965).

> When one party is clearly wrong, it will eventually give way. That is what happened here. They had no business in putting those missiles in and lying to me about it. They were in the wrong and knew it. So, when we stood firm, they had to back down. But this doesn't mean at all that they would back down when they felt they were in the right and had vital interests involved.

F This British cartoon showed how serious the situation had been (November 1962).

Q

1 Why do you think the US people were not told the full details of the agreement to remove the Soviet missiles?
2 a) How do sources G and H disagree?
   b) Suggest reasons why each took their view.
3 What evidence is there that people believed the Cuban crisis might cause a nuclear war?

8

Vietnam

In the 19th century, the French had added a huge part of South East Asia to their empire. This area was known as Indo-China. During the Second World War, Japanese troops occupied the area. Local people did not want to be ruled by foreigners so they organised resistance groups. One of them was the Viet Minh. It was a mainly communist group, led by Ho Chi Minh.

Japan surrendered on August 15 1945; in September, Ho Chi Minh announced that Vietnam was an independent republic. The Second World War was over – but the 20th century's longest war was about to begin.

The French wanted to keep Vietnam in their empire and French troops returned to southern Vietnam. Ho Chi Minh's Viet Minh was not going to let the French re-take Vietnam without a fight. In 1946, war broke out between the French and the Viet Minh.

The USA did not approve of France fighting to get its colony back. However, between 1946 and 1954, the USA gave over $1 billion to France to help them win. The USA gave all this money because they were afraid that communism would spread through South East Asia. This idea was known as the 'domino theory'.

A US President Eisenhower explained it in 1954:

You have a row of dominoes set up. You knock over the first one. What will happen to the last one is the certainty that it will go over very quickly. Asia has already lost some 450 millions of its peoples to communist dictatorship. We simply can't afford greater losses.

B The domino theory: what the USA feared would happen in South East Asia.

Despite all the money, the French lost. In 1953, they tried to trap the Viet Minh by setting up a camp at Dien Bien Phu. The Viet Minh surrounded it and set up gun positions on the nearby hills: the French could not get supplies into the camp.

From March to May 1954, the Viet Minh besieged Dien Bien Phu. After two months, the French were defeated and the survivors were put in prison camps. Another two months later, an armistice was signed and the French agreed to leave Indo-China. There had been 16500 French troops at Dien Bien Phu; only 3000 lived to tell the story.

Vietnam divided

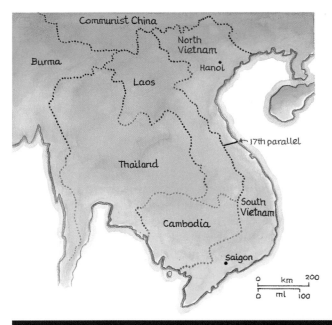

C South East Asia, showing Vietnam divided.

The peace talks were held at Geneva. It was agreed that Vietnam would be split into two parts, along the line of the 17th parallel. The north became a communist republic, controlled by the Viet Minh. In 1955, southern Vietnam, too, became a republic, with Ngo Dinh Diem as president. The plan was that an election for the whole country would be held two years later and the country would be united.

However, many of the South Vietnamese also supported Ho Chi Minh. An election would turn the whole of Vietnam into a communist country. So the USA promised to support the South Vietnamese government and the South Vietnamese refused to take part in an election.

Why did the USA get involved?

Ho Chi Minh wanted a united, communist Vietnam. The USA believed that he was being supported by the Chinese to turn the whole of South East Asia communist. President Eisenhower (1953-61) believed in the domino theory: if South Vietnam became communist, Laos and Cambodia might be the next targets.

So the USA supported Diem's government of South Vietnam, based in Saigon. It was mainly made up of rich Roman Catholic landowners. Diem's rule was harsh and his government was unpopular with the peasants, many of whom were Buddhists.

His government was also corrupt. The Americans sent money to help Diem's government; much of it was used to bribe Diem's friends. The USA sent arms, too: some of them were even sold to the communists.

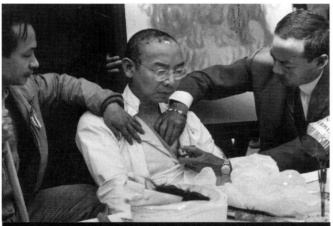

D Buddhists were persecuted by Diem's government and tried to draw the world's attention to Vietnam. This professor decided to write to the UN with his own blood (1963).

1960–63

By 1960, whole areas of South Vietnam were in open rebellion. That same year, the National Liberation Front (NLF) was set up to oppose Diem; its members were mostly communist and received help from North Vietnam. The South Vietnamese government called them the Vietcong. A civil war was developing between the government and its peasant opponents.

President Kennedy (1961–3) became very concerned. American money and arms had not saved the South Vietnamese government. So he decided to send more advisers, as well. By November 1963, about 10 000 US advisers were helping South Vietnamese troops.

E This Buddhist monk chose to protest by committing suicide (1963).

Meanwhile, the South Vietnamese army tortured and executed thousands of peasants in an attempt to destroy the NLF. This made the peasants even more determined to fight back. In November 1963, Diem's hated government was overthrown and Diem was killed. Outside the palace in Saigon, crowds celebrated.

> Ho Chi Minh means 'Ho, the Seeker of Light'. The North Vietnamese called him 'Uncle Ho': he had no title. His costume included sandals made from old motorcycle tyres.

Full-scale US war

Later that month, Kennedy himself was assassinated. The new president was Lyndon Johnson. He decided to increase American help to the South Vietnamese. The US Navy patrolled the Vietnamese coast on the look-out for NLF soldiers. In August 1964, the North Vietnamese retaliated and attacked an American destroyer in the Gulf of Tonkin.

Johnson already had secret plans to escalate the war but could not carry them out unless he could show there was a reason to do so. The Tonkin incident gave him the excuse he needed. The US Congress passed a resolution which allowed Johnson to fight a war against the North Vietnamese. It was a decision which many Americans would later regret.

Q

1 a) Why did the French fight in Vietnam?
  b) Why did the Americans fight in Vietnam?
2 a) President Diem's government was corrupt. Does that mean that the USA was wrong to support Diem?
  b) Would it have been right if his government had been honest and fair? Give reasons.
3 Why do you think neither Kennedy nor Johnson simply pulled out of the war?

THE TONKIN RESOLUTION (1964)

The Tonkin Resolution opened the floodgates for US involvement in Vietnam. It allowed President Johnson to use US troops to defend any SEATO country. It allowed US aircraft to bomb North Vietnamese naval bases and oil refineries; Johnson believed it allowed him to fight a full-scale war in Vietnam and that is what he did.

The first US marines arrived in South Vietnam early in 1965; by the end of the year, there were 150 000 US troops in the country. By 1969, the number had risen to half a million.

A President Johnson, speaking in 1965:

Most of the non-communist nations of Asia cannot, by themselves, resist the growing might and ambition of Asian communism. If we are driven from the field in Vietnam, then no nation can ever again have the same confidence in American promises or American protection. In each land the forces of independence would be weakened. An Asia so threatened by communist domination would [endanger] the security of the United States itself.

B US marines in Vietnam.

American tactic: bombs

Johnson believed that he had to stop the North Vietnamese supplying weapons to the NLF. Therefore, the US air force bombed strategic targets in North Vietnam. They included army bases, factories, railways and bridges. By early 1966, US planes were flying 164 flying missions a day on average. The bombs often missed their target: school children and hospital patients were among those killed.

The weight of bombs dropped on North Vietnam was greater than that dropped by the US air force in the entire Second World War.

American tactic: strategic hamlets

The second strategy had been introduced by President Kennedy. The USA knew that the NLF was supported by most of South Vietnam's peasants. Advisers believed the USA had a better chance of winning if they could stop the peasants from keeping in touch with the NLF.

So US troops turned the peasants out of their own villages and put them in 'strategic hamlets'. These were areas surrounded by barbed wire and controlled by the Americans. About 40 per cent of the Vietnamese population was moved in this way. The scheme made the Vietnamese hate the Americans even more.

C The Ho Chi Minh Trail.

NLF tactic: guerrilla warfare

The USA believed it could win because it had the most modern fighting equipment. The NLF had no aircraft, no tanks and no artillery. What they had instead was experience in fighting a guerrilla war against the French from 1946 to 1954. They used the same tactics against the Americans.

The NLF avoided fighting the US troops in open battle because the Americans were better-armed. Instead, they hid in the jungle or mingled with peasants in the rice-fields.

It was impossible for American troops to know who was a guerrilla and who was not. The NLF wore no uniform so they looked just like the peasants; they spoke the same language so they sounded just like peasants. Indeed, many of them had been peasants so they knew every detail of the jungle.

NLF guerrillas hid in a system of tunnels which stretched for 200 miles under South Vietnam. They launched hit-and-run raids from one tunnel, just 20 miles from Saigon. There was even an underground hospital system. The doctor in charge amputated limbs without anaesthetics and carried out brain surgery with an electric drill.

American tactic: chemicals

Both the USSR and China supplied money and weapons to the NLF. The North Vietnamese brought these weapons through the jungle at night on foot or by bicycle. The most famous route was nicknamed the Ho Chi Minh Trail. One problem for the Americans was that they could not see the people supplying the NLF because the jungle was too dense.

So the Americans dropped chemical bombs to destroy the trees. The result was defoliation – the leaves were stripped from the trees, allowing US helicopters to spot the enemy more easily. Napalm was also used in fire bombs and flame-throwers. It is a thick liquid, which usually contains petrol. It cleared the undergrowth but it also stuck to human beings and burned away their flesh.

D These children were victims of a napalm bomb.

E Ho Chi Minh wrote to President Johnson in 1967.

The US government has committed war crimes, crimes against peace and against mankind. Half a million US troops have [used] the most inhuman weapons and the most *barbarous* methods of warfare, such as napalm, chemicals and gases, to massacre our [countrymen], destroy crops and raze villages to the ground.

Opposition to war

In South Vietnam, innocent men, women and children were burned by napalm and civilians began to doubt whether the USA was really on their side. Increasingly, South Vietnamese people saw the NLF as their friends and their own government as the enemy. US troops became more and more unpopular.

Opposition also grew in the United States. At first, most protests had been from students. But a **draft law** forced young men to go and fight in Vietnam. Black Americans were against it because draft laws hit them hardest. About 12 per cent of

Americans were black but the per centage of draftees who were black was 16 per cent.

Many middle-class Americans were also against the war. By 1967, the death rate had risen to 160 American deaths a week. American parents did not want their sons to die far from home in a war they did not understand.

In January 1968, the NLF launched the Tet offensive, capturing 75 per cent of the main towns in South Vietnam. Even the American Embassy in the capital Saigon was captured for a few hours.

In the end, the offensive failed but the campaign had two important effects.

First, it convinced the Americans that this was a war they could not win. By 1968, more Americans opposed the Vietnam War than supported it. So, second, President Johnson stopped bombing North Vietnam in return for peace talks in Paris. Nevertheless, the number of American dead passed 30 000 by the end of the year.

F This Vietnamese woman is mourning over the remains of her husband, killed during the Tet offensive (1968).

Q

1 Draw a timeline to show events in the Vietnam War. Cover the years 1945 to 1975. Include all the events mentioned on pages 22–25.
2 a) Describe the tactics used by each side and explain why they were used.
   b) Why might American tactics anger (i) the Vietnamese people and (ii) Americans back home?
3 Which photograph do you think would have most shocked Americans? Give reasons.

THE END OF THE WAR

B This picture shows the execution of an NLF officer. It created a big impact in the USA in 1968.

Vietnamisation (1969)

The war made President Johnson so unpopular that he decided not to stand for re-election in 1968. The new president, Richard Nixon, introduced a new policy called Vietnamization. What this meant was that he would go on supplying arms and money to South Vietnam – but the South Vietnamese would do the fighting. As a result, many US troops were pulled out of the country. By 1971, the number had been halved.

However, Nixon did not want the communists to win so he began bombing North Vietnam once more. In 1969, he even began secretly bombing Cambodia to stop supplies being sent to the NLF down the Ho Chi Minh Trail. These bombing raids were kept secret even from the US **Congress**: military records showed 'nil' raids on Cambodia and bombing records were burned.

In the following year, Laos also became an American target. And, at Christmas 1972, the US dropped 100 000 bombs on Haiphong in North Vietnam: it was the greatest bombing raid in history.

Nixon wanted a way out of the war but he wanted 'peace with honour'. The man who supplied it was his foreign affairs adviser, Dr Henry Kissinger. He held secret talks with the North Vietnamese, even while the bombing and fighting continued. Indeed, the bombing was partly to persuade Americans that North Vietnam was being forced to give up.

It took four years before the two sides could agree. An armistice was finally signed at Paris in January 1973 and American troops went home. Thousands of South Vietnamese went with them, including many politicians who knew they were wanted by the communists. Kissinger's reward was the 1973 Nobel Peace Prize, which he shared with a Vietnamese delegate at the peace talks.

C Since the war thousands of refugees have left Vietnam.

1973–75

There had been peace talks; there had been an agreement. But there was little peace. The fighting dragged on for two more years, with the communists gradually winning. In April 1975, the NLF captured Saigon. They renamed it Ho Chi Minh City in honour of their leader who had died in 1969.

US advisers left the city in such a rush that there was no time to burn the files which listed their Vietnamese secret agents. To the outside world, it did not look like 'peace with honour'.

The war's effects

1 The domino theory

President Kennedy had been afraid that, if Vietnam became communist, so would the rest of South East Asia. This happened in both Laos and Cambodia. However, it did not happen in Thailand, Burma or Malaysia. The domino theory had been proved wrong.

2 Vietnam

Vietnam was united in 1976 but the country had been destroyed by bombing. Tropical rainforest had been reduced to scrubland; large areas of farming land were little more than a wasteland.

Vietnam's economy was also destroyed. It went from being a major rice exporter to a country that could not feed its own people. After Vietnam was invaded by the Chinese in 1979 it relied on aid from the Soviet Union. Many professional Vietnamese fled the country, looking for safety abroad. Their departure caused more damage to the country's economy.

3 The cost

No one knows how many people died in the war: the total Vietnamese death toll might have been two million. Nearly 58 000 US troops died and another 300 000 were wounded. The war cost the USA $120 billion.

When the peace talks were over, prisoners-of-war were exchanged. But 2400 US troops were still reported as missing in Vietnam. Some Americans believed that some of them were being used as slave labour, 20 years later. One French prisoner was kept like this for 12 years.

4 US bitterness

The small state of North Vietnam had beaten one of the world's superpowers. It was a war that many Americans wished to forget. Long afterwards, many relatives of dead **GIs** still blamed the politicians for sending their sons and husbands to Vietnam in the first place. They were also bitter about the 'draft dodgers' – the well-off young men who managed to avoid going to fight. Not a single member of the US Congress lost a son in the war.

D The remains of a crashed US B-52 bomber in Vietnam (1989).

Historians look back

As more sources become available, historians are reaching new conclusions about the war. In 1968, people believed that the Tet offensive was a North Vietnamese success. It convinced many Americans that they could not win the war. Today, we know that the NLF themselves thought it was a failure. They lost many of their key fighters during the campaign.

Some historians doubt whether American public opinion really had a major impact on what the government did. When the build-up of troops was slowed down in 1969, the government was more worried about the cost of the war than what Americans thought. The American public generally still thought that the country should keep fighting, as long as there was a chance of winning.

Finally, people used to think that the USA's military might could not win against the NLF's guerrilla tactics. But there is evidence that the USA's position improved between 1968 and 1972. As so often in history, it is not what happened that mattered. What counted was what people thought was happening.

E Shirley Judges: *Superpower Rivalry* (1994).

Some 700 000 veterans, women as well as men, have suffered psychological effects: it has been shown that they are far more likely than the rest of the population to experience panic attacks, depression, drug addiction and to be divorced or unemployed.

F Philip Jacobson, describes the effect of the war

Excessive drinking and/or drug abuse, emotional instability, trouble with the law: all are symptoms of the [distress] that has driven some 250 000 veterans to seek treatment. [But] drug abuse among veterans is not significantly higher than among groups who did not serve, and they are less likely than non-veterans to go to jail.

Q

1 a) Why did Nixon want to end the war?
   b) How successful was this end, from the American point of view?
2 a) How did the war affect Vietnam?
   b) How did the war affect the USA?
   c) For which side were the effects worse? Give reasons.
3 a) Study sources E and F. Do they agree or not? Give reasons.
   b) Why is it difficult to reach conclusions about the Vietnam War?

Czechoslovakia (1968)

In 1956, Soviet tanks had crushed the uprising in Hungary. This action showed that the USSR would not tolerate countries in eastern Europe who wanted to go their own way. It was 1968 before another communist country tried to win some independence from the USSR. This time, it was Czechoslovakia.

Czechoslovakia had been a democratic country before World War II. Its standard of living had been high. Even under communist control, it was more industrialized than most of the satellite states. However, its economic achievements were not as great as its people hoped.

The country was suffering from severe **inflation** and people complained that it was being exploited by the Soviet Union. There were student protests and criticism of the Czech Communist Party.

In January 1968, a new man was chosen as First Secretary of the Communist Party. His name was Alexander Dubcek. He wanted to improve the economy. He planned to do this by:

- having less central planning
- making more contacts with the West
- modernizing the Communist Party itself.

These changes would make Czechoslovakia very different to other communist countries so he tried to reassure the USSR. He told Soviet leaders that Czechoslovakia would not leave the Warsaw Pact.

Dubcek called his plans 'socialism with a human face'. The Czechoslovak people discussed politics openly for the first time in years. People called it 'the Prague Spring': it was as if the nation were being reborn.

B April 1968: Svoboda, the Czech president (holding a hat) stands beside Alexander Dubcek (to his left) outside the cathedral in Prague.

The Czech people supported Dubcek's reforms. So did Yugoslavia and Romania but the USSR did not. Soviet leaders tried to persuade Dubcek to give up his reforms. They were afraid that Czechoslovakia might leave the Warsaw Pact, whatever Dubcek said. They were also worried about the effect his changes might have on other communist countries.

The Prague Spring gave way to early summer. Soviet politicians continued to talk to Dubcek. Meanwhile, behind the scenes, they planned to invade Czechoslovakia, just as they had invaded Hungary in 1956. In early May, Soviet tanks began moving through Poland and East Germany towards Czechoslovakia. By late July, about 75 000 Soviet troops were in position just outside the Czechoslovakian border.

In July, the USSR and four other Warsaw Pact countries sent a message to Dubcek. In effect, they asked him to change his policy. He did not. Dubcek did not believe the USSR would invade Czechoslovakia; nor did Tito, who visited the country in August.

A Dubcek's reforms (1968):

- **freedom of assembly**
- **freedom of religion**
- **political prisoners freed**
- **trade unions allowed**
- **freedom to travel to the West**
- **limits on the powers of the security police**
- **press censorship to end**
- **a new National Assembly would be elected, in which communists would not have all the power**

C Dubcek described his thoughts at this moment in *Hope Dies Last* (1993).

I thought that we could [win] against the Soviets because in the end their bullying would not exceed certain limits. The 1956 crushing of Hungary was way behind us: they would not repeat that. Most of the world agreed.

He was wrong.

According to the USSR, what happened next was that they received a letter from leading Czech communists. It asked for Soviet help in putting down a counter-revolution. (No one is sure whether this is true or whether the letter was made up.)

On the night of 20–21 August 1968, Soviet troops entered Czechoslovakia. There were also a few troops from Poland, Bulgaria, Hungary and East Germany to make it look like a Warsaw Pact joint exercise.

One Czech official who saw them thought they were shooting a film: he did not believe his country was being invaded. Most Czechs did not resist because they knew there was no point: they could not hope to win. Faced with Soviet rifles, they placed flowers in the barrels.

However, some fought back. Barricades were set up in the streets and tanks were blown up. Students tore down street names to confuse the invaders. Anti-Soviet broadcasters stayed on the air by moving from one hiding place to another.

Meanwhile, Dubcek had been arrested and taken to Moscow where he was forced to sign an agreement, ending most of his reforms. He returned to Czechoslovakia but could not bring the Czech resistance under control. In April 1969, he was forced out of office and a pro-Soviet leader called Gustav Husák took over. He clamped down on all opposition inside the country.

In 1991, it was revealed that one Czech in every 100 had been a secret service agent under the communists.

D Czech protestor on a Soviet tank (21 August 1968).

E Look at source B. Spot the difference. This photograph was used in Czechoslovakia after 1969.

Why did the USSR send in troops?

F The official Soviet version was given by Tass, the Soviet news agency, 21 August 1968.

Party and government leaders of the Czechoslovak Socialist Republic have asked the Soviet Union and other states to give brotherly help to the Czechoslovak people with armed forces. This request was brought about by the threat from counter-revolutionary forces. The troops will be withdrawn as soon as the threat to Czechoslovakia and neighbouring communist countries has been eliminated.

G The official Czech version was given by the Czechoslovak Communist Party on Radio Prague, 21 August 1968.

Yesterday, troops of the Soviet Union, Polish People's Republic, East Germany, the Hungarian People's Republic and the Bulgarian People's Republic crossed the frontiers of the Czechoslovak Socialist Republic. This happened without the knowledge of the president, the chairman of the National Assembly, the premier or the first secretary of the Czechoslovak Communist Party.

Q

1 a) Why did Dubcek reform Czechoslovakia?
  b) Why would his reforms have worried the USSR?
  c) Why did the USSR invade Czechoslovakia?
2 a) How can you tell that the invasion was the USSR's idea and not a Warsaw Pact exercise?
  b) Study sources F and G and compare them with the text. Which source do you think is correct? Give reasons.
3 a) How was source B changed?
  b) Why do you think it was changed?

Détente

A Czech youths protesting about the invasion.

Leonid Brezhnev, the Soviet leader, stated that it was the duty of any communist country to intervene with force in any other communist country which was threatened by capitalists. This applied even to independent countries. This policy became known as the Brezhnev Doctrine.

In practice, it meant that the USSR would stop any country in the Warsaw Pact which tried to go its own way. Soviet troops had succeeded in controlling Hungary in 1956. Afterwards, Hungarian living standards had gone up and its leaders seemed popular. The Czech invasion of 1968 tried to repeat this success. It seemed as if Soviet policy had changed little in 12 years: resistance would still be crushed.

However, the invasion of Czechoslovakia marked a turning-point in the Cold War, though few people knew it at the time. What happened in Hungary was not repeated in Czechoslovakia. The Czech people never really trusted those who replaced Dubcek. And the Brezhnev Doctrine was almost an admission that countries would only stay communist if the USSR forced them to do so.

Also, the USSR's reputation among other communists was damaged by its treatment of Czechoslovakia. The Romanian leader made a speech, attacking the Soviet action. President Tito of Yugoslavia also condemned it. So did the Chinese. There was criticism from communist parties in Britain, France, Italy and Spain.

Moves toward détente

The Czech crisis had occurred when East-West relations were improving. From 1964 onwards, politicians talked about **détente** between East and West. Détente means a relaxing of tension.

At first, it seemed as though events in Czechoslovakia would put an end to détente. Many countries felt that they needed to strengthen their defences against a possible Soviet attack. For instance, President Tito increased the Yugoslav armed forces.

However, there were good reasons why détente continued. The Cuban crisis had shown just how dangerous a confrontation could be. Neither side wanted the next disagreement to turn into a nuclear war. Each side already had enough nuclear weapons to destroy the other. Better relations meant that fewer weapons needed to be built. This not only saved money: it allowed western and eastern leaders to portray themselves as peace-makers.

Both the USA and USSR wanted détente because each had economic problems during the 1970s. In the USA, there was rising inflation. Money spent on nuclear weapons meant there was less available to improve living conditions for poor Americans.

The USSR, too, faced problems. It was spending 20 per cent of its budget on defence. Also, its industry was very inefficient compared with American industry. Soviet industry had to improve before its leaders could raise their people's standard of living.

Lastly, there were political reasons for détente. The USSR had begun to quarrel with communist China, her huge neighbour to the south. Meanwhile, the Americans had become bogged down in the Vietnam War.

Test Ban Treaty (1967) Banned nuclear tests in space

Nuclear Non-Proliferation Treaty (1968) between USA and USSR (later joined by other nations) This tried to stop smaller countries making nuclear weapons

NOT FOR YOU

BANNED

B Two agreements of the 1960s.

So, throughout the late 1960s and 1970s, American and Soviet leaders tried hard to reduce tension. This led to better trade links between the two superpowers after 1972. In particular, the USA sold its surplus wheat cheaply to the USSR. However, the biggest benefits of détente were agreements to limit missiles.

C US President Nixon and Breznev (1974).

SALT I

Richard Nixon became US President in 1969. Both he and Brezhnev wished to improve relations between the USA and the USSR. In 1969, they made the first real attempt to limit weapons when they began the Strategic Arms Limitation Talks (SALT). These talks were concerned with expensive middle-range nuclear weapons.

Meanwhile, Nixon tried to improve relations with China. In 1971, he agreed to let China join the UN. In February 1972, he visited the Chinese capital, Beijing. Soviet leaders became frightened that the USA and China might ally against the USSR.

In May 1972, Nixon visited the Soviet Union. He was the first American president to go there since Roosevelt went to Yalta in 1945. In Moscow, the two superpowers signed the SALT 1 Treaty. They agreed to limit building certain missiles for five years. However, this agreement did not reduce existing stocks of weapons.

Helsinki Agreement (1975)

This agreement was another product of détente. Both sides officially accepted the existing borders between European countries. The leaders also agreed a Declaration of Human Rights - rights which each country promised to give their people.

They included:

- freedom of speech
- freedom of religion
- freedom of movement
- freedom from unfair arrest

In effect, western leaders accepted that the USSR would continue to rule over communist eastern Europe. Soviet leaders were delighted with this. In return, they made half-hearted promises about civil rights which they did not intend to keep. While the talks went on, new Soviet medium-range missiles were secretly being put in position. They were aimed at western Europe.

Was communism winning?

The mid-1970s were the high point of détente. But the USSR's real aim had not changed: it wanted to defeat capitalism and turn the whole world communist. Soviet leaders believed they were succeeding.

The USA's defeat in Vietnam was just one sign that capitalism seemed to be losing: Cambodia and Laos, as well as Vietnam, turned communist. In Africa, too, support for communism was growing.

SALT II

Despite SALT I, the number of Soviet and American missiles increased during the 1970s. A later American President, Jimmy Carter (1977–81), wanted both sides to get rid of nuclear weapons completely and more SALT talks were held.

A new SALT agreement was signed by Presidents Carter and Brezhnev in June 1979. This limited the number of long-range missiles, especially those with multiple warheads. But, in December, Soviet troops invaded Afghanistan. The SALT talks stopped abruptly and the US Congress refused to **ratify** the SALT II agreement. Détente was over.

Q

1 What were: (a) the Brezhnev Doctrine, (b) SALT I and (c) the Helsinki Agreement?
2 a) What were the reasons for détente?
  b) Why would (i) the West and (ii) the USSR feel pleased with the Helsinki Agreement?
3 a) How did the events on these two pages help to lessen the Cold War?
  b) What evidence is there that the Cold War was really still going on?

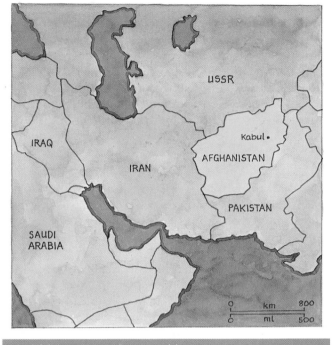

A Afghanistan and its neighbouring countries.

The Brezhnev Doctrine was widely attacked. Yet the criticism did not stop Brezhnev using force in Afghanistan, 11 years after Czechoslovakia.

During 1979, Afghanistan became very unsettled. Muslim opposition groups attacked the new Afghan government which was both non-Muslim and pro-Soviet. The USSR looked on uneasily. It, too, had a large Muslim population in the areas nearest to Afghanistan. Soviet leaders were worried that extremist Muslim ideas might soon affect the Soviet Union itself.

What happened next was a textbook example of how the USSR dealt with difficult neighbours. On 28 December 1979, Soviet leader Brezhnev phoned US President Jimmy Carter with some news. He told him that Soviet troops had been invited into Afghanistan to protect the country from outside attacks.

In fact, Soviet troops were already in Afghanistan. The airport at Kabul, Afghanistan's capital, had been captured on Christmas Eve, to allow the USSR to bring in troops and equipment. At the same time, Soviet troops had crossed the northern border into Afghanistan.

A KGB squad attacked the palace in Kabul and **assassinated** the communist president, Hafizollah Amin. On New Year's Day 1980, a new government was set up in Kabul, led by Babrak Karmal. He was a former Afghan leader who had been in exile in the USSR. A Soviet plane had flown him back specially to take over the government.

Criticism of the invasion was worldwide. Afghanistan's Muslim neighbours, Pakistan and Iran, both objected. So did western powers. The USA **boycotted** the 1980 Olympic Games in Moscow as a protest. That same year, Ronald Reagan was elected as the next US President after demanding that the United States build more nuclear weapons.

The USSR ignored the protests and its troops stayed. By February 1980, there were 80 000 of them. However, they soon found that putting down opposition in Afghanistan was much less easy than in Hungary or Czechoslovakia.

B An Afghan boy and his mother collecting scrap from ruined houses (1995).

Soviet troops were supposed to support the Afghan army against the Muslim groups which were anti-communist. But they faced two problems. First, the Afghan army was not as good as they had believed. Second, they faced opposition from rebel forces, called the mujaheddin.

These rebels were not just fighting to get rid of Soviet troops. They were fighting to turn Afghanistan into a Muslim country. They were well-equipped because they were given weapons by both the USA and China, who opposed the Soviet invasion.

The mujaheddin fought a guerrilla war against the Soviet and Afghan armies. Soviet troops controlled the towns where they were based but the mujaheddin controlled the countryside. They attacked Soviet supply routes; they shot at Soviet transport planes.

C These boys fought for the Mujaheddin rebel forces. One of them is holding an AK-47 rifle.

D Alex Bovin, writing in *Izvestia*, a Soviet newspaper (1980).

> The Soviet Union was forced to make a choice: we had to bring in troops or let the Afghan revolution be defeated. We knew that the decision to bring in troops would not be popular, even if it was legal. But we also knew that we would have ceased to be a great power if we [did not take] unpopular but necessary decisions.

E One Russian mother tried to discover how her soldier son died. She was told:

> You cannot walk around saying that your son has been killed in Afghanistan. That's classified (secret) information.

F Aless Adamovich, writing in *Moscow News*, a Russian newspaper (1990).

> The Afghan people lost a million lives in a war which we had no right to get involved in. We couldn't defeat the Afghan 'bandits' because they were fighting us as invaders.

G One Soviet soldier who fought in Afghanistan said afterwards:

> We were given medals which we don't wear. When the time comes we'll return them. Those medals [were] received honestly in a dishonest war.

Other nations increased their pressure on the Soviet Union. The USA, for instance, banned grain exports to the USSR. In 1971, the UN General Assembly asked the USSR to leave Afghanistan: the request was ignored.

Despite this, the USSR faced problems. Muslim nations, which had once been friendly, turned hostile. The USSR increasingly became worried that Muslims inside the Soviet Union might revolt. In any case, the war grew unpopular as Soviet casualties increased.

In 1985, a new Soviet leader, Mikhail Gorbachev, decided to withdraw from Afghanistan. Agreement was reached in Geneva in 1988 and the last Soviet soldiers left Afghanistan in February 1989. Over 20 000 Soviet troops had died in ten years of fighting.

The consequences were far greater for Afghanistan itself. About a million Afghans may have died – and the fighting went on even after the Soviet departure. By 1989, almost half the original Afghan population had become refugees. Those who were left could no longer grow enough food because the war had destroyed so much farmland.

Q

1. a) Why did the USSR get involved in Afghanistan?
   b) How was it similar to Soviet takeovers of other countries?
   c) Why was it not successful?
2. What do you think the soldier in source G meant by 'dishonest war'?
3. a) Read sources D and F. How do they disagree?
   b) How does sources F disagree with what Brezhnev told Carter in 1979?
4. What evidence is there that Russians regretted their involvement in Afghanistan?

In 1980, Americans elected Ronald Reagan as their new president. It seemed as though détente was over – and it was, for a while. Reagan was determined to stand up to the USSR, which he called 'the evil empire'. He decided to deploy Cruise and Pershing missiles in Europe. These were intermediate-range missiles which could not be spotted by enemy radar.

Despite this, the USA and USSR began new arms talks at Geneva in July 1982. The new ones were called START (Strategic Arms Reduction Talks). The two sides discussed limiting intermediate nuclear weapons in Europe.

Meanwhile, Reagan had increased American spending on defence. In the early 1980s, the USA was spending over a trillion dollars on its military budget. In 1983, US scientists began work on a new project – the Strategic Defence Initiative (SDI). The plan was to build a laser shield around the USA which would have made it impossible for Soviet missiles to hit American targets. People nicknamed it 'Star Wars'.

This plan frightened the Soviets because it would have changed the balance of power. Both the USA and the USSR were equally vulnerable to long-range missile strikes; 'Star Wars' would have ended that. In 1983, the Soviet delegation walked out of the START talks.

Many Europeans were worried, too. If the USA were protected by 'Star Wars', a Soviet attack on Europe was more likely. The American missiles stationed in Europe were an obvious target for Soviet missiles. There might be a 'limited' nuclear war – limited to Europe.

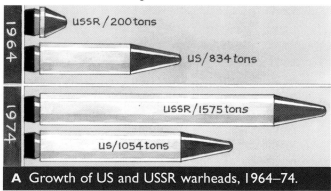

A Growth of US and USSR warheads, 1964–74.

Nuclear missiles were not President Reagan's only answer to the 'evil empire'. He was also making secret plans to destroy the USSR's 'empire' once and for all, starting with Poland.

Poland was a good choice. The Poles had disliked the Russians for at least two centuries. Also, the Roman Catholic Church was a powerful force in the country. About 80 per cent of Poles were Catholic. From 1945 onwards, the Church had reminded people that communism was not the only thing to believe in.

By 1980, the Polish economy was in serious trouble. Workers went on strike as a protest at high prices, and food and fuel shortages. At the ship-yard in Gdansk, workers demanded pay rises and improved benefits. They also wanted the right to form a free trade union which could negotiate working conditions with the government.

B Gdansk strikers at prayer, August 1980.

Their wish was granted: in August, Poland became the first eastern communist country to have a free trade union. It was called Solidarity. The leader of its ten million members was Lech Walesa. The USSR did not send troops in, partly because of world criticism of its invasion of Afghanistan. Also, late in 1980, the USA warned Brezhnev that, if the USSR invaded Poland, the USA would sell weapons to China.

But Soviet leaders were worried and ordered a crackdown on the protesters. In December 1981, the Polish armed forces took over the government and General Jaruzelski became Polish leader. Riot police moved in with water cannon and troops used tear gas to break up meetings. Solidarity's leaders were put in prison. In 1982, the union was banned.

That might have been the end of the matter, but in June 1982 a unique meeting took place between US President Reagan and Pope John Paul II. He had become Pope in 1978 and he was Polish.

C Ronald Reagan, speaking in the 1990s:

We both felt that a great mistake had been made at Yalta and something should be done. Solidarity was the very weapon for bringing this about, because it was an organisation of the labourers of Poland.

The two men believed they could work together to keep Solidarity alive. They planned to do it by secretly undermining the Polish government. An American adviser described it as 'one of the great secret alliances of all time'.

They believed that, as a result, the USSR would lose its grip on Poland and the country could regain its freedom. If Poland became free, other communist states might follow.

From 1982 to 1989, various western organisations provided money to help the banned union. Some of it came from the CIA. Solidarity also received equipment, smuggled into Poland by priests and foreign unions. It included telephones, transmitters, computers and video cameras.

Above all, Solidarity received advice on how to deal with the Polish government and the USSR. This advice was based on secret information which the USA received from Polish priests and even spies in the Polish government.

However, helping Solidarity was only one aspect of Reagan's policies. It was part of an overall plan to weaken the USSR's economy and force reforms inside the USSR and eastern Europe.
Reagan was hugely popular in the USA. In 1984, he was re-elected president in one of the biggest victories in American history. However, his strategy was an expensive one. His massive spending on arms had run up huge debts and Reagan somehow had to cut costs. What he needed were more talks on arms cuts.

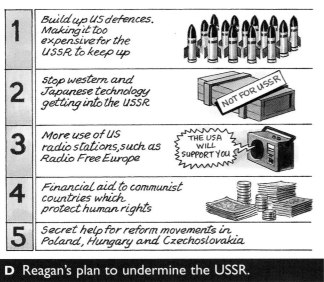

1	Build up US defences. Making it too expensive for the USSR to keep up
2	Stop western and Japanese technology getting into the USSR
3	More use of US radio stations, such as Radio Free Europe
4	Financial aid to communist countries which protect human rights
5	Secret help for reform movements in Poland, Hungary and Czechoslovakia

D Reagan's plan to undermine the USSR.

E Solidarity used equipment supplied by the CIA to break into Polish radio and TV programmes. In 1992, a Catholic official recalled one occasion.

There was a great moment at the half time of the national soccer championship. Just as the whistle sounded, a 'SOLIDARITY LIVES!' banner went up on the screen and a tape came on calling for resistance. What was [clever] was waiting for the half-time break.

In 1985, history came to his aid. A new Soviet leader, called Mikhail Gorbachev, was chosen. He, too, was in charge of a country which was spending huge sums on defence which it could not afford. (In the 1970s, the USSR had spent 20 per cent of its budget on defence.) Gorbachev needed to cut costs so Soviet industry could make more consumer products.

A Soviet report of 1983 had said that the Soviet economy was not working – and could not work without huge changes. There had to be more small businesses and co-operatives; people needed to be given greater freedom. The country needed to be more democratic.

It was a radical plan but Gorbachev used it as the basis for his new policies. He called these *glasnost* (openness) and *perestroika* (renewal). He wanted Soviet people to speak more openly and he encouraged Soviet leaders to listen to criticism.

The scene was set for some of the most unexpected dramas of the 20th century.

In 1981, women set up a 'peace camp' at the US air base at Greenham Common. They were protesting at NATO's decision to site 96 Cruise missiles there.

Q

1 What were the following: Cruise missiles; 'Star Wars', START; glasnost; perestroika?
2 a) Read source C. What 'mistake' did Reagan think had been made at Yalta?
   b) Look at Reagan's plan (source D). What results do you think he hoped each action would have?
   c) What overall effects might these have on the USSR?
   d) Explain carefully why Gorbachev also wanted arms reductions.

MIKHAIL GORBACHEV

The Soviet economy was in a bad state when Gorbachev took over. Soviet leaders boasted that there was no inflation; in fact, there was - but no one knew how much. Official figures about the economy were false – but hardly anyone knew what the real ones were.

Industrial production was falling and up to 70 per cent of it was for military use. The military budget was out of control: no one really knew how much the armed forces cost. The communist system was corrupt – and no one knew how much that cost, either.

Gorbachev needed arms cuts for two reasons. First, the USSR needed to spend less on defence and more on reforms at home. Second, Reagan had announced the Star Wars project in 1983. The USSR responded in two ways: it increased its defence budget and it carried out its own research on Star Wars.

They discovered an unpleasant truth: their technology was so far behind the USA's that they could not compete. There was really only one solution. As a leading communist said, 'They had to drop out of the arms race'.

> In 1981, an American computer failure led to a message, suggesting that there was a nuclear attack on the USA. 100 B-52 bombers were made ready for take-off to drop nuclear bombs.

Arms agreement (1987)

Gorbachev came to power in March 1985. In November, he met Reagan in Geneva. The two leaders agreed in principle to cut offensive weapons by 50 per cent. They would also try to limit medium-range missiles. 'The world has become a safer place,' Gorbachev told reporters afterwards.

It was a promising start. But the 1986 summit in Iceland broke down over Star Wars which the USA refused to give up. However, Gorbachev confirmed that the USSR would withdraw from Afghanistan and promised that the USSR would not test any more nuclear weapons in the atmosphere unless the USA did so.

Success eventually came in December 1987 when the two leaders agreed to get rid of all medium- and short-range nuclear weapons. Reagan formally signed the treaty on a visit to the Kremlin. It was an amazing turnaround. He had been determined to stand up to the communists. Now, he signed the first agreement with them to reduce nuclear weapons. The dismantling of these weapons began at once.

A US experts watching Soviet troops destroying nuclear weapons (1988).

B President Reagan, speaking in 1988 (TV film).

I told [Mr Gorbachev], 'We don't mistrust each other because... we're armed this way. We're armed this way because we mistrust each other. And if you and I can eliminate the reasons for this mistrust, the arms will take care of themselves.

However, there had been arms agreements before but the Cold War had gone on. This time was different because Gorbachev had other plans. Arms cuts saved money but they did not solve the USSR's economic problems. And solving those, it turned out, was to end the Cold War in a dramatic fashion.

A Soviet report of 1983 had said that the Soviet economy was not working - and could not work without huge changes. There had to be more small businesses and co-operatives; people needed to be given greater freedom. The country needed to be more democratic.

It was a radical plan but Gorbachev used it as the basis for his new policies. He called these *glasnost* (openness) and *perestroika* (renewal). He wanted Soviet people to speak more openly and he encouraged Soviet leaders to listen to criticism.

In 1985, Gorbachev believed these two policies would reform the Soviet system. If corruption could be stamped out and everyone did their job properly, communism could be made to work. He soon discovered that he was wrong.

Gorbachev wanted *perestroika*: he wished to rebuild the Soviet state. He eventually realised that this meant radical reforms in the Communist Party, too. However, he may not have realised how many people wanted to go further and get rid of the Communist Party altogether.

This was especially true elsewhere in eastern Europe. The policy of *glasnost* encouraged people to criticise the system - the communist system. In the USSR's satellite countries, people deeply disliked both their own communist leaders and Soviet interference. In Hungary and Czechoslovakia, many people had bitter memories of how Soviet tanks had destroyed their attempts at freedom.

D Gorbachev and Reagan in Moscow's Red Square (1988).

E This poster represents workers as bees producing honey (money).

In March 1986, a crowd of 3000 marched through the streets of Budapest. It was led by teenagers carrying the Hungarian flag. They were celebrating Hungary's unofficial independence day. (The communists had stopped celebrating this after World War II.) They demanded more democracy. At first, the police left them alone but, that evening, they used truncheons to beat up demon-

There was, of course, another way to save communism: tanks. The USSR had used them in Hungary in 1956 and Czechoslovakia in 1968. The question in many people's minds was: would Gorbachev, too, use tanks to stop people gaining their freedom?

The answer, they discovered, was 'no'. And, once again, Poland led the way in finding out.

Q

1 a) Why did Gorbachev need arms cuts?
   b) Who do you think he was keen to get the USA to give up Star Wars?
   c) Read source B. Do you agree with Reagan? Explain your answer.
2 a) What was the link between the Soviet economy and glasnost?
   b) How did glasnost affect eastern Europe?
3 a) According to source C, why didn't Gorbachev's reforms work?
   b) Why would this failure affect the Cold War?

POLAND (1982–9)

When the USSR did not invade Poland in 1980, it was another turning-point in the Cold War. But Poland's path to democracy over the next ten years was not a smooth one. Solidarity was banned in October 1982, although prisoners were released soon afterwards. The Pope played a key part in achieving this.

In return for promising to visit his native Poland, Pope John Paul II insisted that:

- **martial law** should end
- prisoners should be released
- there should be independent trade unions.

Poland's leader, General Jaruzelski, introduced reforms to improve the economy and began to work more closely with the Catholic Church. Meanwhile, support for the Communist Party was falling: half of its members left. Those who stayed in the party were mostly Catholics and many read the underground newspapers. They were not Lenin's idea of typical communists.

A Solidarity's advice to workers to help create chaos (1982).

The effect of Gorbachev

Both the Polish government and Solidarity supported Gorbachev's reforms. Indeed, the union had wanted these reforms for some years. The communists were anxious to show they supported Gorbachev because they wanted to hold on to power.

But the government had become weak. At the first sign of opposition, it was willing to change its policies.

B Spot the food: queues got longer and even basic goods were more difficult to find (1981).

C One Polish politician said:

> Nothing ever happens. You make a proposal, then the trade unions oppose it. The security police report discontent, and it's withdrawn.

However, something was happening to the Polish economy: it was getting worse. Prices were rising and living standards were falling. The country owed huge sums of money abroad and could not afford to replace old industrial machinery. Production was falling. In 1988, an opinion poll showed that about a quarter of Poles wanted to emigrate to the West.

In January 1988, there were more strikes in protest at Poland's poor economic record. Workers demanded that Solidarity should be made legal again. Lech Walesa asked for talks with the government and the government agreed.

D Walesa told those at the talks:

> There is only one direction. It must go towards a democratic system, towards the rule of law and the freedom of its citizens. Even if we cannot get all that, we have to start somewhere.

The talks lasted for two months. In April 1989, a deal was struck: Solidarity would be made legal and workers would have the right to strike. More important, there would be new elections. Two-thirds of the seats in the *Sejm* (parliament) would be guaranteed for communists and their allies; one-third could be contested by other parties.

Of course, the system was designed so that the communists would win. Despite this, it was an historic decision: the government had agreed to hold free elections for the first time since the war. They were also the first free elections in any communist country.

When the election was held, Solidarity won all 161 seats open to opposition parties. This left Poland in a strange position: the communists did not have the people's support; Solidarity did not have enough MPs to run the country. In effect, the communist leadership stayed in control.

But not for long. Jaruzelski (now President) tried to get Solidarity to join a coalition government but Walesa refused. Instead, two weeks later, Solidarity formed a coalition with two other parties and won a majority of votes in the *Sejm*.

The following day, Jaruzelski appointed a new government, which included Solidarity MPs. The new prime minister was Tadeusz Mazowiecki, a non-communist and Roman Catholic. It was the first non-communist Polish government since the Second World War - and the first in any Soviet satellite.

E August 1989: (from left) Lech Walesa and Prime Minister Tadeusz Mazowiecki.

Effect on the Cold War

The Cold War had happened partly because the USSR and USA had very different systems – communism and capitalism. To defend their views, each side had built up huge amounts of weapons. And each side had its supporters – the USA was supported by western Europe while the USSR was supported by eastern Europe.

But this situation was changing. Both sides had already agreed to arms cuts. If eastern Europe rejected communism, another reason for the 'war' would have disappeared. In the summer of 1989, Poland did reject communism – and Hungary was not far behind.

Hungary

In May 1988, Karoly Grosz took over from János Kádár as Communist Party leader and there were big changes in the Party leadership. In January 1989, the government decided to rebury Imre Nagy. Days later, it announced that an enquiry into the events of 1956 had shown that it had not been a 'counter-revolution', after all. They decided that it had actually been a popular uprising.

Early in 1989, it was agreed that other political parties should be allowed. Instead of sending in tanks to stop this, Gorbachev did the opposite: he agreed to start withdrawing troops from Hungary.

Why?

When Gorbachev came to power, he knew that the USSR had to find new ways of dealing with eastern Europe. So he abandoned the Brezhnev Doctrine. In future, east Europeans would be treated as partners. The USSR would not send in tanks; instead, Gorbachev believed that each country should sort out its own problems.

F Gennady Gerasimov, one of Gorbachev's advisers, explained the new policy in autumn 1989.

> The new doctrine is Frank Sinatra's doctrine. Frank Sinatra has a very popular song, 'I had it my way'. So Hungary, Poland, any other countries has it its own way. They decide which road to take. It's their business.

Q

1 Study source A. Explain why Solidarity gave each piece of advice.
2 a) What mistakes did the Polish Communist Party make?
    b) Take any one of Solidarity's actions and explain why it was clever.
3 a) How did what happened in Hungary in 1989 differ from what happened in Hungary in 1956?
    b) Why did the USSR act differently?
4 Some people think that the major turning-point in eastern Europe was in 1980 when the USSR decided not to invade Poland. Do you agree? Explain your answer, using pages 38–9.

1989–91: The End of Communism

The Berlin Wall destroyed (1989)

In May 1989, Hungary took down the barbed wire fence along its Austrian border: people could now travel from East to West. About 20 000 East Germans fled to the West before the border was officially opened in September. The East German leader, Erich Honecker, tried to hold back the tide and stay in power. But, without Soviet support, there was little he could do and he resigned in October.

The Berlin Wall had been built to keep East Germans inside East Germany. Oddly, it came down for the same reason. The East Berlin communist leader announced that it would be opened on 9 November. At midnight on 8–9 November, thousands celebrated as the gates were opened. People hacked at the wall with pickaxes to take home a souvenir. The Iron Curtain's most famous landmark would soon be just a heap of rubble.

B The photos people never expected to see (number 2): Ronald Reagan speaking below the bust of Lenin in 1988.

A The photos people never expected to see (number 1): the Berlin Wall is torn down (1989).

The rest of communist Europe could not avoid the effects. On 10 November, the Bulgarian president resigned after holding power for 33 years. Later that month, demonstrations in Czechoslovakia toppled the communist government without bloodshed.

By contrast, the revolution in Romania was a violent affair. A civil war raged for four days between the Romanian army and supporters of Nicolae Ceausescu, the country's unpopular president. Eventually, he was captured and executed by firing squad on Christmas Day 1989.

The end of the Cold War

Reagan retired in 1989 as the most popular president in American history. The new president, George Bush, met Gorbachev on December 3 1989. They made an historic announcement: the Cold War was over.

However, changes continued to sweep through eastern Europe during 1990. In March, talks began in Berlin on the **reunification** of East and West Germany. Britain, France, the USA and USSR later signed a treaty which gave back full powers to East and West Germany as independent nations. In October, they were reunited after 45 years. Meanwhile, East Berlin's History Museum locked up the display which covered the years 1949–61.

THE IRON CURTAIN
Certificate of origin

[Hungarian text on certificate, partially legible]

C The pictures people never expected to see (number 3): Hungary sold its part of the Iron Curtain as souvenirs.

D Liliya Shevtsova, writing in *Moscow News* (February 1990).

The first free elections will soon be held in all the neighbouring countries. It is already safe to say that the Communist Parties will not remain the ruling parties. The principles behind [Communist Party] activities, its central structure and its *monopoly* on power – all [are against] the requirements of democracy. Such a party [cannot] be reformed.

In April 1990, communist rule in Hungary ended when voters chose the Hungarian Democratic Forum to lead the new government. Yugoslavia, too, held its first multi-party elections that month. Even Albania took its first steps towards the end of communist rule when the ban on opposition parties was ended in December. In the summer of 1991, they actually joined the government.

START Treaty signed (1991)

In August, Gorbachev and Bush finally signed START after nine years of talks. They agreed to destroy about one-third of their nuclear weapons. They signed the agreement with pens made from scrapped missiles.

The end of the USSR (1991)

In August 1991, there was an attempted **coup** against Mikhail Gorbachev by hard-line communists. It failed mainly because the new Russian President, Boris Yeltsin, opposed it. He urged soldiers to mutiny and workers to strike in protest. Thousands took to the Moscow streets.

Just four days later, Yeltsin suspended the Communist Party in Russia. As one Russian wrote to a Soviet newspaper, 'The world has moved on. The Party didn't make good use of 72 years.'

After the coup failed, many Soviet republics decided they wanted to be independent and not controlled by Moscow. One of them was Russia itself, led by Boris Yeltsin. In December, the Soviet state finally broke up. Gorbachev resigned as Soviet President, as there was no longer a Soviet state to preside over.

As he announced his resignation on television, the communist red flag was lowered for the last time over the Kremlin. Gorbachev said, 'The old system fell apart before the new one began to work.' The 'evil empire' which Reagan had wanted to destroy, had destroyed itself.

E The pictures people never expected to see (number 4): Gorbachev speaking in 1992 in Fulton, Missouri, where Churchill first spoke of an 'Iron Curtain' in 1946.

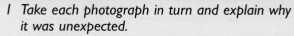

1 Take each photograph in turn and explain why it was unexpected.
2 a) Why did source D say that the communists would lose power?
 b) Why did Gorbachev think the communists lost power?
 c) Why do you think the communists lost power?

THE COLD WAR'S LEGACY

As the Iron Curtain tumbled, so the secrets came spilling out. For instance, in 1991, Gorbachev and Bush agreed to take nuclear bombers off alert and put nuclear warheads in storage.

It sounded very impressive. It seemed to reduce the risk of nuclear war. In fact, there was nothing new in this agreement. The arrangement had secretly existed for decades.

Accidents in the USA in 1966 and 1968 had led to all American bombers being grounded until the end of the Cold War. Soviet planes had never carried nuclear weapons for safety reasons. For years, they had been loading up dummy ones!

START II signed (1993)

In 1993, Yeltsin and Bush signed the START II Treaty which brought further cuts in the stocks of US and Russian missiles. However, it still left both countries with about one-third of their long-range warheads – over 6000 of them.

Yet the risk of nuclear war remained because nuclear missiles still existed – not just in the USSR and the USA but in many smaller countries, too.

Nationalism

The decline of communism led to the return of an old danger. **Nationalism**. Throughout the communist bloc, many people were not satisfied with democracy: they wanted their own independent nation too.

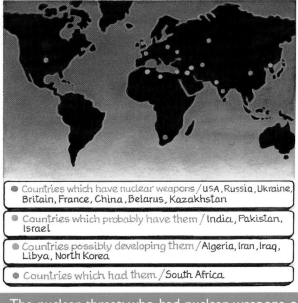

- Countries which have nuclear weapons / USA, Russia, Ukraine, Britain, France, China, Belarus, Kazakhstan
- Countries which probably have them / India, Pakistan, Israel
- Countries possibly developing them / Algeria, Iran, Iraq, Libya, North Korea
- Countries which had them / South Africa

A The nuclear threat: who had nuclear weapons or could make them (1993).

Latvia, Estonia and Lithuania all became independent in 1991 and joined the United Nations. On January 1 1993, Czechoslovakia peacefully split to become the two separate states of the Czech Republic and Slovakia.

In the former USSR, fighting broke out as a number of areas tried to win independence. However, the worst violence occurred in what had been Yugoslavia. Tito had held together an explosive mixture of Serbs, Croats and Muslims but communist control collapsed in 1990. The following year, the Serbs refused to accept a Croat as leader and both Slovenia and Croatia declared independence.

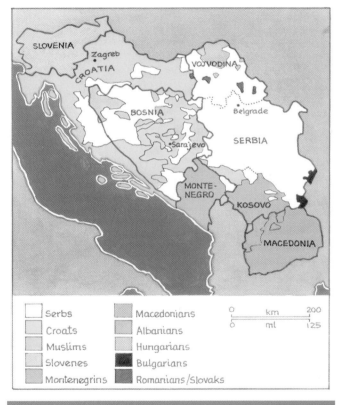

- Serbs
- Croats
- Muslims
- Slovenes
- Montenegrins
- Macedonians
- Albanians
- Hungarians
- Bulgarians
- Romanians / Slovaks

B Who controlled what in the former Yugoslavia (1992). The situation changed regularly.

During the civil war which followed, the Serbian government used a policy which they called 'ethnic cleansing'. This meant removing non-Serbs from mainly Serb areas – or killing them. Apart from the deaths, up to 20 000 Muslim and Croat women and girls were raped.

The United Nations agreed a ceasefire in Croatia in 1992. It was the first of many in the region but 40 000 UN troops have failed to keep the peace. As the fighting continued in 1995, a solution seemed no nearer. One Serb soldier gave this chilling warning: 'The time of living together is over.'

Korea

Korea was one of the Cold War's first trouble spots. It is also one of the last. North Korea remains communist whilst South Korea is capitalist. Anti-aircraft guns in Seoul, the South Korean capital, are still permanently guarded, ready for a North Korean attack.

A narrow demilitarised zone separates the two sides. Every day at noon, both sides meet there to settle disputes, such as shooting incidents.

Vietnam

In 1993, the French President said that the French had made a 'mistake' in fighting in Vietnam. In the USA, the arguments about American involvement in Vietnam go on. Robert McNamara was US Defence Secretary under Presidents Kennedy and Johnson. In 1995, he admitted that his handling of the war had been 'terribly wrong'.

It led to a new round of arguments about the war. The USA has not forgotten Vietnam because it has not yet recovered from the experience. Vietnam was the war the Americans lost. What many still wonder is whether they should have been fighting in the first place. On the other hand, many Americans argue that the USA lost the war in Vietnam – but won the battle against communism.

> **C** Artyom Dobrovolsky is a taxi driver in Moscow. In 1993, he told an American magazine:
>
> This country reminds me of a huge, filthy market, where everyone sells and everyone is for sale. I understand the reforms are for the better, and I understand that everyone has a right to buy and sell. But the sight is repulsive. I see old women peddling jars of mayonnaise, and I feel pity and anger and shame all at once.

D A beggar sits near a dollar sign in Moscow (1995).

Eastern Europe

What about the people of eastern Europe? Are they satisfied with their new lives? A poll early in 1993 showed that over half the people in the former USSR thought they had been better off under communism. About 70 per cent in eastern Europe were not satisfied with democracy. And 10 per cent wanted to emigrate to the West.

The Cold War's cost

> **E** Mikhail Kapitsa was Soviet Deputy Foreign Minister in the 1980s. In 1995, he said:
>
> This *ideology* costed us billions and billions and billions. Billions for nothing. Billions for just ideas which practically nobody observed. And finally we've stopped observing.

It is impossible to say what the Cold War cost. Billions of dollars and roubles were spent on building nuclear weapons. Defence budgets in the USA and USSR soaked up money which might have been used to improve living standards. Now that the Cold War is over, many more billions are being spent on getting rid of these weapons.

Nor have all the debts been paid yet. Putting East Germany on a par with West Germany may take up to 20 years; the bill will be about $100 billion every year. The cost of sorting out the ex-USSR's economy has been estimated at nearly $2 trillion a year. However much help the West gives, the Russians and others will have to pay for most of it on their own.

However, the first half of the 20th century saw two world wars. In the second half, there has been none. Some people believe that this was partly because both superpowers had nuclear weapons – but were afraid to use them.

> **Q**
>
> 1 a) What is nationalism?
>   b) Why has it led to fighting since communism collapsed?
> 2 Who might have benefited if there had been no Cold War? Explain your answer in detail.
> 3 'Nuclear weapons prevented World War III.' Do you agree? Give a detailed answer.

Afterword

Afghanistan Fighting still continued in 1995.

Atom bomb It was revealed in 1994 that four of the main nine inventors of the atom bomb gave information to the USSR about it in the years after 1945.

Baltic States Latvia, Estonia and Lithuania became independent in 1991 and joined the UN.

Berlin The allied occupying troops finally left Berlin in 1994. The British HQ, originally built for the 1936 Olympics, is a rare surviving complete example of Nazi architecture. It is protected by a preservation order.

Berlin Wall Most of the 224 000 tons of concrete panels were ground down and sold as building materials. However, 100 metres of it was bought by the New York Museum of Modern Art. Another section now stands outside CIA head quarters.

Czechoslovakia Czechoslovakia split to become the two separate states of Slovakia and the Czech Republic on January 1 1993

Alexander Dubcek In 1989, Dubcek was elected President of the Czech Parliament after the Czech revolution. In 1990, he was received at the Kremlin by Gorbachev. He died after a car crash in 1992. Many people were suspicious about the circumstances of his death. General Salgovic, the man who arrested him in 1968, committed suicide soon after the 1989 Czech revolution.

Erich Honecker The former East German leader was put on trial in 1992 for the manslaughter of people who had died trying to cross the Berlin Wall. The charges were dropped on humanitarian grounds.

Korea Anti-aircraft guns in Seoul, South Korea, are still permanently manned, ready for a North Korean attack. There is a daily meeting in the demilitarised zone to settle disputes. Under a 1994 agreement, North Korea gave up its nuclear programme in return for two nuclear reactors and free fuel oil. Kim Il Sung, North Korean dictator and the world's longest-serving political leader, died in the same year.

Imre Nagy In June 1989, Imre Nagy's body was reburied, along with four others. A sixth coffin was empty – it represented all the others who died in the 1956 revolution. Three weeks later, the Hungarian Supreme Court ruled that Nagy had been innocent.

North Vietnam The USA established formal links with North Vietnam in 1995, 20 years after they left South Vietnam.

Poland The body of Paderewski, Poland's first Prime Minister, who died in New York in 1941, was reburied in Warsaw in 1992.

Russia It is now possible to buy pictures of nuclear sites from the Defence Ministry for $1500. Low-grade secrets are also for sale.
In 1994, Queen Elizabeth II visited Russia. She was the first reigning British monarch to do so.

Saigon The US Embassy in Saigon is now partly occupied by the Vietnam State Petroleum Company. The helicopter landing pad on the roof is still marked out, with the letter H in the centre. It was from there that the last Americans in South Vietnam were airlifted in 1975.

Vietnam War By 1995, US investigators had received proof that most missing US servicemen were dead. Only 55 remained to be traced.

Warsaw Pact This was dissolved in 1991. Since then, Poland, Hungary, Lithuania, the Czech Republic and Slovakia have all applied to join NATO.

Yugoslavia The end of communist rule in Yugoslavia was not as peaceful as in Czechoslovakia. Civil war broke out in 1991 and was continuing in 1995.